Jon

The Effective Teacher's G
Moderate, Severe and Pro
Difficulties (Cognitive Imp

This updated second edition of *The Effective Teacher's Guide to Moderate, Severe and Profound Learning Difficulties (Cognitive Impairments)* has been restructured and expanded to ensure it continues to meet the needs of the busy teacher.

This new edition is highly relevant and contextualised, drawing on the curriculum and assessment, pedagogy, resources, therapy and care, and school and classroom organisation. It is accessible and practical in approach, yet offers the necessary underpinning of research and professional knowledge to enable the teacher to be self-critical in developing classroom approaches.

The book accessibly and thoroughly discusses the classroom difficulties associated with:

- mild cognitive impairment
- moderate to severe cognitive impairment
- profound cognitive impairment
- conditions associated with cognitive impairment.

A much-needed source of knowledge for teachers, students on initial teacher training courses, school managers and administrators, this book will be of interest to anyone who supports children and young people with cognitive impairments.

Michael Farrell is a widely published private special education consultant. He works with children, families, schools, local authorities, voluntary organisations, universities and government ministries. He has published books extensively with Routledge, with recent titles including *The Special Education Handbook: An A–Z Guide,* 4th edition, and *Debating Special Education.*

The Effective Teacher's Guides Series, all by Michael Farrell

The Effective Teacher's Guide to Behavioural and Emotional Disorders: Disruptive behaviour disorders, anxiety disorders and depressive disorders, and attention deficit hyperactivity disorder, 2nd edition
PB: 978-0-415-56568-4 (Published 2010)

The Effective Teacher's Guide to Sensory and Physical Impairments: Sensory, orthopaedic, motor and health impairments, and traumatic brain injury, 2nd edition
PB: 978-0-415-56565-3 (Published 2010)

The Effective Teacher's Guide to Autism and Communication Difficulties, 2nd edition
PB: 978-0-415-69383-7 (Published 2012)

The Effective Teacher's Guide to Dyslexia and other Specific Learning Difficulties (Learning Disabilities), 2nd edition
PB: 978-0-415-69385-1 (Published 2012)

The Effective Teacher's Guide to Moderate, Severe and Profound Learning Difficulties (Cognitive Impairments), 2nd edition
PB: 978-0-415-69387-5 (Published 2012)

The Effective Teacher's Guide to Moderate, Severe and Profound Learning Difficulties (Cognitive Impairments)

Practical strategies

Second edition

Michael Farrell

LONDON AND NEW YORK

First published 2006 by Routledge
This second edition published 2012
by Routledge
2 Park Square, Milton Park, Abingdon, Oxon OX14 4RN

Simultaneously published in the USA and Canada
by Routledge
711 Third Avenue, New York, NY 10017

*Routledge is an imprint of the Taylor & Francis Group,
an informa business*

British Library Cataloguing in Publication Data
A catalogue record for this book is available from the British Library

Library of Congress Cataloging in Publication Data
Farrell, Michael, 1948
The effective teachers guide to moderate, severe and profound
learning difficulties (cognitive impairments): practical strategies/
Michael Farrell. – 2nd ed.
p. cm.
1. Autistic children – Education. 2. Autistic children – Language.
3. Autism in children. 4. Communicative disorders in children. I. Title.
LC4717.F37 2012
371.94 – dc23
2011025393

ISBN: 978-0-415-69386-8 (hbk)
ISBN: 978-0-415-69387-5 (pbk)
ISBN: 978-0-203-15283-6 (ebk)

Typeset in Bembo
by Taylor & Francis Books

MIX
Paper from
responsible sources
FSC
www.fsc.org   FSC® C004839

Printed and bound in Great Britain by
CPI Antony Rowe, Chippenham, Wiltshire

Contents

The author

Michael Farrell was educated in the United Kingdom. After training as a teacher at Bishop Grosseteste College, Lincoln, and obtaining an honours degree from Nottingham University, he gained a Masters Degree in Education and Psychology from the Institute of Education, London University. Subsequently, he carried out research for a Master of Philosophy degree at the Institute of Psychiatry, Maudsley Hospital, London, and for a Doctor of Philosophy degree under the auspices of the Medical Research Council Cognitive Development Unit and London University.

Professionally, Michael Farrell worked as a head teacher, a lecturer at London University and as a local authority inspector. He managed a national psychometric project for City University, London, and directed a national initial teacher-training project for the United Kingdom Government Department of Education. His present role as a private special education consultant includes work with children and families, schools, local authorities, voluntary organisations, universities and government ministries.

His many books, translated into European and Asian languages, include:

- *Foundations of Special Education: An Introduction* (Wiley, 2009)
- *The Special Education Handbook: An A–Z Guide,* 4th edition (David Fulton, 2009)
- *Debating Special Education* (Routledge, 2010)

Preface

I am of course extremely pleased to be writing the preface to the second edition of this book, *The Effective Teacher's Guide to Moderate, Severe and Profound Learning Difficulties (Cognitive Impairments).*

It was previously called *The Effective Teacher's Guide to Moderate, Severe and Profound Learning Difficulties: Practical Strategies,* published in 2006. The first edition attracted favourable comment and I have listened to the views of readers about how the edition might be improved and I have modified the book accordingly. These comments have come from individuals who have contacted me directly and from delegates at conferences I have led, and I am grateful to those who have taken the time to make these suggestions.

I hope the book continues to be useful and I again welcome comments from readers to ensure any future editions are as informative and helpful as possible.

Michael Farrell
Herefordshire
September 2011
dr.m.j.farrell@btopenworld.com

Chapter 1

Introduction

This chapter sets the book in the context of the series of which it forms a part. It explains the features of the new edition. I outline the types of disorders with which the book is concerned and provide preliminary information that will be helpful when reading later chapters. The chapter describes the content of subsequent chapters and suggests potential readers likely to find the book useful.

The Effective Teacher's Guides

The Effective Teacher's Guides published by Routledge concern different types of disabilities and disorders. These include cognitive impairment ('learning difficulties' in the United Kingdom and 'mental retardation' in the United States of America), autism, emotional and behavioural disorders, reading disorder/dyslexia and others. Each book in the series describes practical strategies that enable the educational progress and psychosocial development of pupils with particular disabilities and disorders.

The titles are:

- *The Effective Teacher's Guide to Behavioural and Emotional Disorders: Disruptive behaviour disorders, anxiety disorders and depressive disorders, and attention deficit hyperactivity disorder* (2nd edition);
- *The Effective Teacher's Guide to Sensory and Physical Impairments: Sensory, orthopaedic, motor and health impairments, and traumatic brain injury* (2nd edition);
- *The Effective Teacher's Guide to Autism and Communication Difficulties* (2nd edition);
- *The Effective Teacher's Guide to Moderate, Severe and Profound Learning Difficulties (Cognitive Impairment)* (2nd edition);
- *The Effective Teacher's Guide to Dyslexia and other Learning Difficulties (Learning Disabilities)* (2nd edition).

The new edition

The Effective Teacher's Guide to Moderate, Severe and Profound Learning Difficulties (Cognitive Impairments) is the second edition of a book previously published in 2006. It was formerly called *The Effective Teacher's Guide to Moderate, Severe and Profound Learning Difficulties: Practical Strategies.*

The first edition was generously reviewed and well received by readers. This new edition seeks to make the content more widely accessible to readers in different countries. The 2006 edition was set within the context of legislation and procedures in the United Kingdom. The new edition focuses more on strategies that work without undue reference to a particular national context. It also includes an extra chapter on different conditions that can lead to cognitive impairment such as Rett syndrome and Down syndrome.

Cognitive impairments

This chapter outlines types of difficulties and disorders with which the book is concerned. These are derived from classifications used in the United States of America and in the United Kingdom. I then outline the contents of the subsequent chapters and describe the proposed readers.

In the United States of America, pupils considered to need special education covered by federal law both have a defined disability; and are considered to need special education because the disability has an adverse educational impact. Categories of disability under federal law as amended in 1997 (20 United States Code 1402, 1997) are reflected in 'designated disability codes' and include the following:

- mentally retarded (coded 1).

Mental retardation is generally divided into 'mild', 'severe to moderate' and 'profound' categories.

In England, a similar classification (Department for Education and Skills, 2005, passim) includes:

- learning difficulty (moderate, severe, profound).

Broadly, mild mental retardation is equivalent to moderate learning difficulties. Moderate to severe mental retardation corresponds to severe learning difficulties. Profound mental retardation is equivalent to profound learning difficulties. Alternative terms to 'mental retardation' include 'cognitive impairment'. This is used in Australia and elsewhere and is sometimes preferred in the United States of America. In the present book, I mainly use the expression 'cognitive impairment' unless referring to research which specifically uses different terms.

Within child and contextual explanations

There is discussion about terms which might suggest that the difficulty is predominantly within child or mainly environmental/contextual. The term 'impairment' is sometimes taken to imply a within child explanation. The phrase 'learning difficulties' is also used, but sometimes the expression 'learning needs' is heard.

However, the word 'needs' raises difficulties. While it might be taken to place greater emphasis on environmental factors, it does not make it clear how the supposed 'needs' arise nor who decides what the needs are. If the needs arise from predominantly within child factors, then the term is merely a euphemism for impairment. Of course, 'need' implies that provision should be made, but this is often a superfluous meaning given that effective provision is the purpose of special education.

Subsequent chapters

Subsequent chapters concern the following topics:

chapter 2: Mild cognitive impairment/moderate learning difficulties;
chapter 3: Moderate to severe cognitive impairment/severe learning difficulties;
chapter 4: Profound cognitive impairment/profound learning difficulties;
chapter 5: Conditions and factors associated with cognitive impairments;
chapter 6: Summary and conclusion.

Each chapter defines and discusses the condition being considered. I then consider provision with regard to: the curriculum and assessment, pedagogy, resources, therapy and care, and school and classroom organisation. The book includes a bibliography and a combined subject and author index.

Proposed readers

I hope readers will include the following:

- teachers and other professionals in mainstream schools, special schools and other settings;
- student teachers and teachers in the early years after qualification;
- parents;

- school managers and administrators;
- anyone interested in provision for children and young people with cognitive impairments.

Key texts

Farrell, M. (2009b) (4th edition) *The Special Education Handbook: An A–Z Guide* London, David Fulton

The book includes entries specific to communication disorders and autism.

Kauffman, J. M. and Hallahan, D. P. (2005) *Special Education: What It Is and Why We Need It* Boston, MA, Pearson/Allyn and Bacon

This introductory but well-argued book sets out the case for special education and explains some of its main features.

Reynolds, C. R. and Fletcher-Janzen, E. (Eds) (2004) (2nd edition) *Concise Encyclopaedia of Special Education: A Reference for the Education of Handicapped and Other Exceptional Children and Adults* Hoboken, NY, John Wiley & Sons

This reference work includes reviews of assessment instruments, biographies, teaching approaches, and overviews of disabilities and disorders.

Chapter 2

Mild cognitive impairment

Introduction

This chapter uses the expression 'mild cognitive impairment', although different terms are used in different countries. In the United States of America the expression 'mild mental retardation' tends to be used, although 'mild cognitive impairment' and 'mild intellectual disability' are alternatives. In England the broadly equivalent term is 'moderate learning difficulties'.

Various issues are the subject of debate in relation to mild cognitive impairment. I first outline some of these issues. The chapter then considers definitions, prevalence, causal factors, and identification and assessment. Under provision, I look at: curriculum and assessment; pedagogy (communication, literacy and numeracy, behavioural, emotional and social development, slower but stimulating pace, concrete learning, and ensuring relevance and generalisation); resources; therapy and organisation.

Some areas of debate

There is debate about the usefulness of the concept of mild cognitive impairment. Teachers and others may place confidence in categorising severe and profound disorders, but may be more circumspect when it comes to mild disorders. This applies also to cognitive impairment. Profound, moderate and severe cognitive impairment seems to be clearly identifiable to many. But mild cognitive impairment raises some difficulties.

Also, the more severe the cognitive impairment, the more likely it is that neurological and physical correlates can be identified. In the case of mild cognitive impairment, any neurological factors are less clear, but there is a correlation with poorer social backgrounds. This is taken by some commentators to indicate that mild cognitive impairment is not a disability or disorder in the sense that there is something that is identifiable within the child that can explain the slower learning. Mild cognitive impairment is seen by those suspicious of within child explanations as a fundamentally socially constructed disability.

It may be accepted that the learning of a child with mild cognitive impairment is slower than that of typical children of the same age. It may also be accepted that this slower learning may relate to predominantly within child factors such as slower processing of information. Even so it is still unclear whether this is owing to poor social and family conditions and whether if these are compensated for the child would start to catch up with other children.

In practical terms, it is likely that the mild cognitive impairment is related to both within child factors and to environment. The implications for provision are similar in many respects whatever the view taken of the relative contribution of child or environment. Where there is strong evidence that the environment is the main reason for slow learning, the school and others are likely to make efforts to support the family in providing good physical and emotional care and in ensuring compensatory provision to try to counter the previously poor levels of stimulation and support.

Despite these reservations, it may still be maintained that efforts to identify mild cognitive impairment can enable provision to be made that can help the child progress educationally, personally and socially. This is especially so where mild cognitive impairment is associated with behavioural difficulties and speech and language difficulties.

Definitions

Definitions of 'mental retardation' in the United States of America

Definitions of mild cognitive impairment take into account intelligence level and functional behaviour. 'Mild mental retardation' is associated in the *Diagnostic and Statistical Manual of Mental Disorders Fourth Edition Text Revision* (DSM-IV-TR) (American Psychiatric Association, 2000, p. 42) with an intelligence quotient (IQ) range of 50/55 to 70. With all levels of mental retardation, whether profound, severe, moderate or mild, IQ levels are interpreted with care, as they are not the sole criterion. Assessing mild cognitive impairment is not a matter of reading off an IQ score and coming to the conclusion that a child has the impairment.

The diagnostic criteria for mental retardation also include 'co current deficits or impairments in present adaptive functioning'. These are in two out of a list of ten areas. The areas are: 'communication, self-care, home living, social/interpersonal skills, use of community resources, self-direction, functional academic skills, work, leisure, health and safety' (American Psychiatric Association, 2000, p. 49).

Broad generalisations are made about the sort of progress children and young people with mild cognitive impairment might make and the areas concerned. Children with mild mental retardation tend to 'develop social and communication skills during the pre-school years (ages 0 to 5 years)' (American Psychiatric Association, 2000, p. 43). They have minimal impairment in sensorimotor areas. By the late teens, they can acquire academic skills up to about sixth grade level.

It has been argued with regard to mild mental retardation (Greenspan, 2006) that there are limitations in an IQ-based definition. One of the reasons for this suggestion is that IQ does not capture the full range of ways of being 'intelligent'. Also there are difficulties with functional-based definitions because they confound mental retardation with other forms of disability. In other words, function may be limited for other reasons than mild cognitive impairment.

For some, the combination of intelligence assessment and functional assessment helps to address the perceived limitations of one or other of the assessments on their own. For others, alternatives are argued to be better. One proposal is to ground a definition in its 'natural taxon', that is a taxonomic group such as a class/classification. This taxon is determined from the behaviours of people widely considered to have mental retardation. Key features are various forms of vulnerability (Greenspan, 2006).

Related to this, in 2002, the American Association on Intellectual and Developmental Disabilities (AAIDD) agreed a supports-based definition. This viewed mental retardation as a condition that can be enhanced by the provision of supports rather than as a more static disability. However, such definitions are not without their own problems. One difficulty is that it is hard to envisage the support supposedly required being allocated fairly unless it is based on some judgement of what is required. This in turn ultimately refers to characteristics of the person who is deemed to require the support. If these are defined according to intelligence level and functional behaviour, the definition has come full circle. If the requirement of support is not based on these usual factors, then other criteria are necessary. What at first looks like an alternative definition begins to look more like an avoidance of how judgements for support are made.

However, the notion of support provision could inform and clarify existing definitions of cognitive impairment. It might also point the way to possible pedagogic approaches. There is still a difficulty of circularity. The individual is given support say in the area of social skills. He is given this support because it is judged that he 'needs' it. The basis on which he needs the support is that his level of social skills is lower than age typical. This is what functional assessment indicated. Therefore, the support is based on criteria that it apparently seeks to avoid.

Definitions of 'moderate learning difficulty' in England

In England, 'moderate learning difficulty' equates broadly with 'mild mental retardation' in the United States of America. Definitions in England wrestle with similar difficulties to those in the United States.

A definition of 'moderate learning difficulties' in England government guidance states that these pupils 'will have attainments significantly below expected levels in most areas of the curriculum, despite appropriate interventions. Their needs will *not* be able to be met by normal differentiation and the flexibilities of the National Curriculum' (Department for Education and Skills, 2005, p. 6, italics added). They 'have much greater difficulty than peers in acquiring basic literacy and numeracy skills and in understanding concepts. They may also have associated speech and language delay, low self-esteem, low levels of concentration and underdeveloped social skills' (ibid. p. 6).

Attainments are low 'despite appropriate interventions' presumably because of the child's 'difficulty' in 'acquiring basic literacy and numeracy skills and in understanding concepts'. The guidance implies the child's home or family circumstances are not one of the factors that constitute 'special educational need' or 'SEN', stating: 'Under-attainment may be an indicator of SEN but poor performance may be due to *other factors* such as problems in the child's home or family circumstances or poor school attendance' (Department for Education and Skills, 2005, p. 2, italics added).

A range of problems is opened up by the use of the expression 'needs will *not* be able to be met' (Department for Education and Skills, 2005, p. 6, italics added). It is not clearly specified in the definition what the supposed 'needs' are or who decides what they are. Neither is it stated how anyone could know when those needs have been met and what the indications are that they have been met. This is a variation of the problems that arise with attempts to use supports-based definitions. The supports are provided to meet a supposed need, but this is not specified. In the England definition, the needs are mentioned but not specified and the support that might be required is not specified either. Euphemism takes the place of attempts to define a condition.

Furthermore, in England there are no nationally agreed criteria for disabilities and disorders. As a consequence, some local authorities try to establish their own definitions and criteria where they can. A definition of 'moderate learning difficulty' in one local authority may differ from that in an adjoining authority. Consequently, research that seeks to establish what works with children with mild cognitive impairment is harder to apply in different local authorities. This is because the definition used by a particular local authority may not correspond with the definition used in the reported research. There have even been local authorities that are reluctant to define mild cognitive impairment at all in case it could be interpreted as negative labelling.

Remembering such caveats, studies in England have indicated that pupils with 'moderate learning difficulties' tend to have other disorders or disabilities too. Pupils with moderate learning difficulties attending special schools were reported by head teachers to have associated difficulties (Male, 1996). The sample comprised 54 special schools in England for pupils with moderate learning difficulties in 1993. Some 87 per cent of head teachers reported that up to half of their pupils had language and communication difficulties, while 80 per cent of head teachers reported that up to half of their pupils had emotional and behavioural difficulties.

A more recent study in the south-west area of England of pupils with 'mild to moderate general learning difficulties' also suggested a high percentage of pupils with other difficulties, including in language and communication (Norwich and Kelly, 2004, pp. 13–14). Where there are such additional difficulties, provision can be modified.

Prevalence

Prevalence for mild cognitive impairment is difficult to establish because of lack of agreement on definitions across countries and within different areas of the same country. It is estimated that of the population with 'mental retardation' the group having 'mild mental retardation' constitute around 85 per cent (with 'moderate mental retardation' accounting for about 10 per cent, 'severe mental retardation' for approximately 3 to 4 per cent and profound for roughly 1 to 2 per cent) (American Psychiatric Association, 2000, p. 43).

Where no biological causation or indeed any other cause can be identified, which is usually the case when the cognitive impairment is milder, more individuals from lower social classes are represented. Different assessments tend to provide different information with regard to different ethnic groups. For example, the *Kaufman Assessment Battery for Children (KABC-II)* (Kaufman and Kaufman, 2004) tends to find smaller discrepancies in the scores of African American and Caucasian children than did an earlier version of the *Wechsler Intelligence Scale for Children (WISC-III)* (Wechsler, 1991).

Care is taken to help ensure that the prevalence for children of different ethnic or cultural backgrounds is reliably and validly determined (American Psychiatric Association, 2000, p. 43). For example, intelligence test procedures use tests in which the individual's relevant characteristics are represented in the standardisation sample of the test. Also the examiner would be familiar with the ethnic and cultural background of the child.

Causal factors

There is debate about the degree to which mild cognitive impairment is attributed to individual or environmental factors and the extent of their interaction. Individual factors are taken to include cognitive impairments as indicated by assessments of cognitive functioning such as intelligence tests and other assessments such as functional ones. The assumption is that outcomes on for example assessments of intelligence are in part reflections of individual differences in cognitive functioning such as memory. Social factors include the possible influence of impoverished social and economic backgrounds that have affected cognitive development.

Remember that earlier, I referred to guidance used in England seeming to indicate that the child's home or family circumstances are not a factor constituting a 'special education need', and that, 'Under-attainment may be an indicator of SEN but poor performance may be due to *other* factors such as problems in the child's home or family circumstances or poor school attendance' (Department for Education and Skills, 2005, p. 2, italics added).

This quotation illustrates the complicated nature of the possible role of family circumstances and the interaction of environmental and 'within child' factors. On the one hand, low attainment may not be the result of predominantly within child difference in cognition, for example, memory functioning. (Such cognitive factors are of course themselves also influenced by the environment.) Low attainment may be related to home and family circumstances. The expectation might be that if family circumstances improved the child would progress better and attain better, perhaps to the level of a typical child of his age.

On the other hand, it may be considered that home and family circumstances have been such that they have influenced (perhaps with other factors) the child's cognitive development. Consequently, even if family circumstances were to change, there would still be evidence of mild cognitive impairment that would not simply evaporate.

Identification and assessment

The identification of pupils with mild cognitive impairment is a challenge for schools and local boards or local authorities because of lack of agreement on definitions. These definitions might include levels of attainment in English and mathematics and other curriculum areas that would be expected (perhaps using percentage cut-off points); or cognitive levels as indicated by standardised tests; or less frequently measures of difficulty in understanding concepts.

Related to this is the debate surrounding the additional use of 'dynamic assessment'. This draws on certain aspects of the work of the Byelorussian psychologist Lev Vygotsky that have become popular in recent years. In particular a 'zone of proximal development' (Vygotsky, 1930 and various dates/1978, p. 86) is cited in which a child learns if tasks are structured to allow him to bridge the space between present unaided functioning and what he can do with support.

Dynamic assessment seeks to measure the responsiveness of an individual to teaching and practice (Bransford et al., 1986). As well as providing a baseline assessment, dynamic assessment offers further information on the degree and form of assistance the child requires in order to reach a higher level of performance and how he responds to such help. This is essentially a preliminary manner of exploring the ways in which a child might learn and develop best.

Provision

Provision for pupils with mild cognitive impairment involves providing a curriculum where subjects are taught at a level which pupils can follow and understand. It also includes the use of approaches that take account of such factors as slower pace of learning and difficulties with concepts. Identifying children with mild cognitive impairment may also attract higher levels of funding, enabling teaching to take place in smaller groups than is typical to encourage better progress and development.

Curriculum and assessment

The curriculum content for pupils with mild cognitive impairment is beyond the usual curriculum flexibilities found in a mainstream school. This is because the level of attainment of pupils with mild cognitive impairment is significantly below that typical of pupils of the same chronological age. The curriculum involves content that is typical of younger children. However, this is presented in a way that takes account of the chronological age of pupils too. The principles are similar to those for teaching adult literacy. The content may be basic, but the interest level is suited to the learner. For pupils with mild cognitive impairment, the level of the content of the curriculum is higher than that for pupils with moderate to severe cognitive impairment.

The curriculum tends to be securely subject based with lessons for literacy/English, numeracy/mathematics, science, history and so on. Communication, literacy, numeracy and personal and social development have particular emphasis in the timetable. This is achieved through allocating more time than is usual in schools and by ensuring these key subjects and skills are embedded in other subjects through cross-curricular planning.

Pupils with mild cognitive impairment have particular difficulty in grasping concepts. Therefore, the curriculum is carefully structured to ensure that knowledge and material is presented in a step-by-step way as far as possible. This helps conceptual understanding to be built on basic practical experiences. Complex topics and procedures are broken down into simpler components. These lead into more complex concepts at higher levels of the curriculum schemes of work.

Consider teaching about the rain cycle. The components may be broken down into parts such as evaporation and condensation. Both of these parts will be conveyed with practical examples and experiences. Only after this practical and experiential foundation has been laid and understood, would the more abstract notion of the rain cycle be approached.

At the same time, the school will make sure the separation of topics into component parts does not distort the whole. The coherence of the curriculum and the way in which practical activities lead into more general applications helps make sure that what the pupil learns is not fragmented. The topics and schemes of work ensure that concepts are revisited in different contexts and are related to everyday experience. Associated resourcing of the curriculum ensures that concrete experiences are given priority. This has implications for pedagogy, as explained in the next section.

Assessment reflects the curriculum content and tends to be related directly to school subjects. Steps of assessment are small enough to ensure that achievements are recognised and celebrated.

Pedagogy

This section concerns approaches to pedagogy that are suitable for pupils with mild cognitive impairment. It covers:

- using concrete objects and developing abstract reasoning;
- communication;

- literacy and numeracy;
- behavioural, emotional and social development;
- self-regulation;
- slower but stimulating pace;
- ensuring relevance and generalisation.

Concrete objects and developing abstract reasoning

Probably the most important aspect of teaching in relation to mild cognitive impairment is helping ensure the pupil is supported in thinking in concrete operations and formal operations as understood in Piaget's theory. These terms are explained below.

Recall that in England, a definition of moderate learning difficulties in government guidance considers these pupils will tend to 'have much greater difficulty than peers in acquiring basic literacy and numeracy skills and in understanding concepts' (Department for Education and Skills, 2005, p. 3).

In Piaget's stage-related theory (Piaget and Inhelder, 1966/1969; Piaget, 1970), cognitive development is seen as gradual and progressive adaptations. These adaptations, for which the child was innately pre-pared, lead to adult reasoning. This process of adaptation involves an interaction between child and environment.

The theory has been modified and developed by 'neo-Piagetian' perspectives (Morra, Gobbo, Marini and Sheese, 2007). These more recent perspectives tend to be informed by neuropsychology and place less emphasis on the logical properties of Piaget's stages and more on the cognitive processing aspects. Challenges have also been made to the view that the stages are determined and are not amenable to acceleration through teaching and enriching the environment.

But aspects of Piaget's work are still illuminating. The stages that concern us here are the:

- concrete operational stage associated in typical development with the ages 7 to 11 years; and
- formal operations stage associated with ages 11 years onwards.

These two stages involve the use of organised systems of interrelated mental actions. They transform reality through 'internalised actions' grouped into 'coherent, reversible systems' (Piaget and Inhelder, 1966/1969, p. 93).

In the concrete operational stage, complex and systematic mental problem solving (using mental representations) can take place in relation to concrete and actual events. A child may know that Peter is taller than David and that David is taller than Jenny. If asked who is smallest, he might work out the answer by mentally picturing Peter, then David, and then Jenny. He would then recognise that Jenny is the smallest. He does not abstract the principle of relative size to reach a solution.

Later, in the formal operations stage, concrete operations develop into new structures enabling the child to reason hypothetically (Piaget and Inhelder, 1966/1969, p. 152). The child becomes able to use the form of logical systems to create and test hypotheses about real or imagined events. For example, he would recognise the inevitability and logical necessity of the implications of relative size in the example of children's heights that we have just considered.

For pupils with mild cognitive impairment, thinking typical of Piaget's stages may develop at later ages than for the majority of children. However, when the pupil does begin to move towards understanding typified by the concrete operational stage, you can reduce his difficulty with abstract concepts. You can do this by using concrete objects and examples to illustrate points. In other words, you can use concrete examples in the physical word to support the cognitively concrete way in which the child thinks through problems.

Mathematical concepts will be illustrated by concrete examples well beyond the chronological age when this might be necessary for pupils without mild cognitive impairment. Time lines may be used to indicate graphically notions of time in history. Physical materials such as number lines and solid shapes will be used in mathematics. While this is necessary with many pupils who do not have cognitive impairment, the regularity and intensity likely to be required for pupils with mild cognitive impairment is greater. Such approaches are also likely to be necessary for longer.

Turning to the formal operations stage, a pupil with mild cognitive impairment may begin to demonstrate thinking typical of this stage much later than other pupils. As the pupil begins to develop this way of thinking, the teacher can structure the use of concrete examples to help the pupil practise and become adept at the abstract manipulations typical of 'formal operations'. Repetition, encouragement, discussion and explanation, far and above what would be required with other children, can help pupils with mild cognitive impairments to begin to reason abstractly. This support is also likely to be necessary to a later age than would be expected for most pupils.

Communication

Developing communication with pupils having mild cognitive impairment addresses speech, grammar, comprehension, meaning and use. A range of strategies to help with these areas are described in the book *The*

Effective Teacher's Guide to Autism and Communication Difficulties, 2nd edition, in this series.

Speech is understood in relation to phonetics, phonology and prosody. To help develop speech, approaches include raising phonological awareness by encouraging interest in and explicit teaching of new vocabulary. Error analysis and articulation exercises may be used to remediate speech sounds.

To help with grammar (syntax and morphology), you might ensure your communication is direct, clear and understandable and that the pupil has extra time and opportunity for over learning as necessary. Planned opportunities for group discussion and the use of visual aids to support communication are other possibilities.

To improve comprehension, you can explicitly teach pupils to maintain attention and to listen well. Other useful strategies are checking specific areas of understanding and encouraging the pupil to make it evident when he does not understand something.

Developing meaning (semantics) may be helped by improving a pupil's skills in and understanding of 'labelling'. This can be done through direct teaching and structured experience using objects and role play, then pictures that represent objects and actions. 'Packaging' is the combination of conceptual and grammatical meaning in communication. It can be improved through using exemplars and models and judiciously reshaping the pupil's utterances. 'Networking' concerns the way in which a lexeme (a lexical language unit of one or more words whose elements do not separately convey the meaning of the whole) gains meaning from its relationship with other words. Networking can be helped by direct teaching in a range of subjects. You can also use and explain key polysemic words (words that have many meanings) in curriculum subjects.

In developing vocabulary, repeated direct experience helps. So, when talking about fruit, you will have real fruits to see, smell, handle and taste. When discussing more abstract terms, such as 'safety', real visual examples of 'safe' and 'unsafe' items and situations will aid the development of the concept. These are examples of the concrete approach to teaching and learning elaborated on in the earlier section. This approach also takes account of the possibility that in family life, there may not have been opportunities to discuss a variety of experiences that contribute to developing a wide vocabulary and understanding.

The use of language (pragmatics) can be aided by developing conversational skills. These skills include introducing a topic, maintaining it and concluding it. This might involve role play and being taught cues used when a conversational partner wants to change or terminate the topic of conversation. The *Social Use of Language Programme* (Rinaldi, 2001) has been employed to promote the communication skills of young people with mild to moderate learning difficulties. It may be used to assess verbal and non-verbal communication skills and to implement an intervention programme.

Literacy and numeracy

Various approaches to literacy have been reported to be effective with pupils having mild cognitive impairment. Two examples are:

- Phonological Awareness Training and
- Reading Intervention.

Phonological Awareness Training (Wilson and Frederickson, 1995) has been experimentally evaluated on a small group of pupils aged 9 to 11 years which included 'some severe learning difficulties and some mild learning difficulties' (Brooks, 2002, p. 106; see also p. 37). The strategy uses a pupil's existing knowledge of letter sounds and words. This helps ensure that new words containing identically written endings present less of a difficulty in reading and spelling.

Also effective was Reading Intervention (Hatcher, 2000). This was evaluated with pupils having 'moderate learning difficulties' having IQ levels of 55 to 75. It uses a combination of phonological training and reading (Brooks, 2002, pp. 38–9, 110). Pupils are helped to isolate phonemes within words to come to recognise that sounds can be common between words and that certain letters can represent specific sounds.

With regard to mathematics, it has been emphasised that the use of concrete and visual apparatus is helpful in teaching pupils with 'moderate learning difficulties' (Panter, 2001). This will include the use of concrete, visual apparatus such as real liquids to measure, real objects to classify, real money to use and real areas to measure.

From such structured experience, the pupil gradually comes to be able to think concretely by visualising items. For example, he can visualise the height of order of three people when told their height relative to one another in pairs. This, as explained earlier, supports thinking at the concrete operations Piagetian stage.

Behavioural, emotional and social development

Cornish and Ross (2003) explain a programme based on a multi-sensory cognitive-behavioural approach to social skills training. This was used in a special school for adolescents having 'moderate learning difficulties'. The aim was to enable pupils to deal with social situations better so they might be transferred part time or full time to mainstream school.

Sessions involved several activities and lasted about 1 hour and 40 minutes each, involving between six and ten students and two adults. Techniques used included rehearsal, modelling and reinforcement to teach students to use speech (internal and external) to influence their behaviour. Acceptable social behaviour and problem-solving skills were taught. The techniques involved verbal instructions, although pictorial cues can also be used.

A little more may be said generally about the techniques that can be used to help behavioural, emotional and social development. Rehearsal simply refers to the practice of a skill or behaviour until it becomes part of the pupil's normal repertoire. The child might practise and rehearse conversational skills.

Modelling has to do with observing the behaviour of a person the child admires and wants to be like. The child then is given the opportunity to try out the behaviour observed for example in role play. For example, this might be used to convey to the pupil different ways of dealing with potential conflict, say, by asking for more information.

Reinforcement refers to a behavioural principle that encourages behaviour that is wanted and discourages behaviour that is not wanted. Rewards are used to increase the occurrence of behaviour considered suitable. Punishments or the withdrawal of expected rewards are used to reduce the likelihood of undesirable behaviour.

More examples of these techniques are to be found in the book *The Effective Teacher's Guide to Behavioural and Emotional Disorders: Disruptive Behaviour Disorders, Anxiety Disorders and Depressive Disorders, and Attention Deficit Hyperactivity Disorder,* 2nd edition, in this series.

Self-regulation

To be able to regulate their behaviour, it is important that pupils are able to develop and evaluate their problem-solving strategies. The teacher's role is central to self-regulatory approaches. You will provide encouragement and structures to enable pupils to develop and evaluate their problem-solving strategies. Borkowski and colleagues (2006) summarise the importance of self-regulation in relation to students with cognitive impairment. This plays a key role in Borkowski's (2000) metacognitive model.

Self-regulation is considered fundamental to most learning problems of individuals with cognitive impairment. Children (and adults) with cognitive impairments often do not use strategies efficiently. They may not suitably generalise newly acquired strategies, perhaps because of immature forms of self-regulation.

Mental planning and monitoring is involved in everyday practical skills from preparing meals to social interaction. Goal orientation is an important aspect. A self-regulated student in a complex learning situation does a range of things. He draws on strategies and sets realistic goals. The student monitors learning progress, adapting strategies to fit the current context and goals (Pintrich, 2000). But individuals with cognitive impairment often experience problems developing these skills. The context and choice of classroom tasks may help increase the self-regulatory functioning of pupils with cognitive impairment.

In examining children's self-regulatory behaviour, Stright and Supplee (2002) compared small-group seat work to teacher-directed instruction. They found that small-group seat work facilitated children's active monitoring.

Also, with regard to literacy teaching for young children, the type of task used by teachers for instruction appears to influence pupils' motivation (Turner, 1995). Open tasks requiring higher-order thinking tend to be more motivating than closed tasks involving memory skills. The teacher or parent might show the pupil skills in self-monitoring. The child may practise these using role play. Then he will be supported to use the self-monitoring skills in different situations and settings such as home and school.

Emotional regulation is strongly linked to the quality of social relationships. More adept emotional regulators enjoy more successful social interactions. The same metacognitive skills needed for intellectual success appear crucial in managing one's emotional states. These skills include being able to recognise emotional states and to move from one emotional state to another to regain equilibrium. Some individuals with cognitive impairments may experience difficulty in forming and developing social relationships partly because of deficiencies in skills relating to emotional regulation (Borkowski et al., 2006).

Language is important in guiding all domains of self-regulation. Internal talk can help self-reflection and inhibit certain responses (Abbeduto & Hesketh, 1997). Children with specific language impairment tend to be rated much lower on teachers' reports of emotional regulation than more typically developing peers (Fujiki, Brinton and Clarke, 2002). In this sense, language abilities and skills lay the groundwork for the emergence of mature forms of emotional and cognitive self-regulation.

Slower but stimulating pace

The pace of learning is a key feature of the education of pupils with mild cognitive impairment. This is because the pupil is likely to have learned at a slower pace than others, leading to lower levels of attainment. In present learning the pupil may respond best to a slower pace of learning than typically developing pupils of the same age. This can help ensure there is time to consolidate learning, over learn and fully understand a learning point.

The pace may be slower, but not so slow that the lesson becomes boring – striking a balance between ensuring learning and keeping interest and enthusiasm. Teachers try to find a pace that ensures learning is secure, but also that the lesson moves along sufficiently to maintain the pupil's interest. This can be fine tuned by strategies of questioning such as a mixture of open and closed questions. Closed questions tend to speed up a lesson; open questions tend to slow the pace. A mixture of the two helps keep a good pace and makes sure pupils have the opportunity to reflect on their learning (through open questions).

Also important is balancing difficult new material to be learned with more familiar material to be consolidated. If the lesson is well structured and progresses from the practical to the more abstract and from the familiar to the less familiar, it is likely that an engaging pace will be sustainable. This is possible because the lesson structure is providing a supportive framework for learning.

An important but pedagogically difficult aspect of pace is that it applies to the pace of a class group and to individual students. Teachers may be good at ensuring a class lesson moves along at a good pace. They may be less good at ensuring individual students work at a suitable pace to ensure good progress. Individual student pace can be increased if necessary by setting time limits for tasks, finding tasks and approaches the student finds motivating, and by encouragement.

Ensuring relevance and generalisation

How do you make teaching and learning relevant? An important way to do this is by drawing out carefully planned and explicitly made connections linked to the pupil's own experience. For example, in making a moving toy, you can ensure pupils engage in a variety of activities. They might talk about their own toys or toys they had when younger. They can watch others play with moving toys. Pupils might examine moving toys and dismantle one to see how it works. Links with other subjects of the curriculum could include English and mathematics. In English lessons pupils can examine toys and learn the names of different toys and their parts. In mathematics they can sort and classify toys and parts of toys, or measure different toys or their parts.

When learning about electricity, you can offer practical experience of making circuits. This can be applied to making a working item such as a doorbell, making comparisons with battery-operated and mains-operated bells. The pupils can study real household accounts for electricity and they can read the electricity meter at home and at school. Where this is linked to real life usefulness it is even better. The meter can be read to give the electricity company the information it needs to charge the school or home the right amount for the electricity used.

Links can be made with mathematics as the students read dials and numerals. Geography can be brought to bear if students visit a generating station or view pylons that carry electricity. Links with personal and social education can include having practical experience of situations in which electricity is used safely.

In subjects such as history, real artefacts will be more pertinent than pictures. In geography real rocks and real ponds are more relevant than books about them. Students might build a pond as part of the school garden. More generally, the teacher will seek to use real items and genuine situations: proper money in real shops, real weather observations, visiting a bank to deposit or withdraw money, writing real letters to post, reading daily newspapers and so on.

Pupils with mild cognitive impairment tend to have difficulties with generalising knowledge and skills (Meese, 2001). Where a task is relevant this can help the pupil generalise knowledge from the situation in which it was learned to new situations. This is because the learning can be related to regularly occurring day-to-day experiences. As well as this, repeated opportunities can be built into the curriculum to develop and apply new skills and knowledge.

Resources

Resources used for pupils with mild cognitive impairment reflect the need to emphasise greatly physical examples to help the development of concrete operations. Resources are also used extensively to help the transition from cognitive development typical of Piaget's concrete operations stage to that typical of formal operations. These resources may include real items instead of pictures. Experiences in and out of school such as visits to geographical features and historical sites are important to provide concrete examples.

These are important for two reasons. The first is that if a child with mild cognitive impairment has limited cultural experiences at home, such visits will be needed to provide experiences, which many other children might have already enjoyed. The second reason is that they will be needed to a much greater degree than is the case for typically developing children, in order for the concepts to develop securely.

Therapy

When discussing definitions earlier, I mentioned that many students with mild cognitive impairment also have communication and language disorders. Where this is so, suitable provision will take this into account. For communication disorders, depending on their severity and complexity, the support of a speech-language pathologist/therapist may be necessary.

Where pupils with mild cognitive impairment have conduct disorders or mood disorders, a range of strategies might be used depending on the circumstances. These include, for children aged 3 to 10 years with disruptive behaviour disorders, the strategies of parent training, social skills training and anger management skills training, problem-solving skills, and classroom contingency management. For adolescents aged 10 to 17 years with disruptive behaviour disorders, provision includes family-based interventions; combination packages of adolescent-focused interventions; and school-based interventions.

Turning to general anxiety disorder, cognitive-behavioural programmes have been used. For obsessive-compulsive disorder, medication, cognitive-behavioural therapy or the two in combination have been employed. Behavioural interventions and cognitive-behavioural therapy have been used with phobias.

With regard to separation anxiety disorder, approaches drawing on group cognitive-behavioural therapy have been applied. For adolescents with mild depressive disorder, cognitive-behavioural therapy for adolescents (with the concurrent treatment of any maternal depression), Interpersonal Therapy Adapted for Adolescents and medication have had positive effects.

Many of these interventions are described in the book *The Effective Teacher's Guide to Behavioural and Emotional Disorders: Disruptive Behaviour Disorders, Anxiety Disorders and Depressive Disorders, and Attention Deficit Hyperactivity Disorder*, 2nd edition, in this series.

School and classroom organisation

The organisation of the classroom for pupils with mild cognitive impairment reflects the slower development of these children. To increase the pace of learning and compensate for possible lack of earlier cultural experiences, the pupils are likely to benefit from teaching in small groups with a high adult to pupil ratio that enables more attention to be given to individuals.

This might be achieved in a special school where all groups tend to be small. It may be achieved in a mainstream school. In a mainstream setting, pupils with mild cognitive impairment may be taught for part of the timetable in a small group in a separate classroom. Alternatively or as well, these students might be taught in small groups within a larger class setting. In larger class settings a student or several students with mild cognitive impairment may be allocated a particular classroom aide or teaching assistant. She will help ensure the tasks are understood and that the pupils are progressing satisfactorily.

Teaching aides sometimes pre-teach aspects of a potentially difficult lesson just before it is due to start. Recapping a lesson after it has finished is another way of ensuring pupils with mild cognitive impairment make the best progress. The timetabling implications of this have to be considered carefully. Also in a mainstream school the teachers and assistants have to be careful that pre-teaching and post-lesson consolidation work does not interfere with the student having sufficient leisure time to make friends and have a break from studying.

In some geographical areas the progress children make in such different settings is monitored and reported to help parents make an informed choice of school. For example, in England, the local authority of Hampshire uses such data (Farrell, 2006, pp. 59–61). Local authority officers, school and parents can make evidence-based judgements about the effectiveness of the different settings in encouraging academic progress and personal and social development. Different settings can learn from each other as they compare the aspects of provision which have promoted good progress and ones that may not have worked so well (ibid.).

Thinking points

Readers may wish to consider with reference to a particular school and local area:

- the extent to which there are suitable criteria for identifying pupils with mild cognitive impairment including any additional difficulties;
- the extent to which practical and relevant activities are used in the curriculum;
- how pedagogy supports the development of thinking typical of 'concrete operations' and later 'formal operations';
- how support for any communication and behavioural and emotional difficulties is ensured.

Key texts

Norwich, B. and Kelly, N. (2004) *Moderate Learning Difficulties and the Future of Inclusion* London, Routledge Falmer

This considers justifications for and limitations of the category of 'moderate learning difficulty'. It examines studies and perspectives relating to inclusion and moderate learning difficulty. The authors report on children's perspectives of their special provision, their perceptions of themselves and how others see them, and of labels associated with 'special educational needs'. They consider social interaction, acceptance and bullying of pupils with moderate learning difficulties. The book discusses possible future strategies.

Switzky, H. N. and Greenspan, S. (2006) (Eds.) *What is Mental Retardation? Ideas for an Evolving Disability in the 21st. Century* Washington, DC, American Association on Intellectual and Developmental Disabilities

This collection of essays includes discussion of the 2002 American Association on Intellectual and Developmental Disabilities (AAIDD) supports-based definition of mental retardation, viewing mental retardation as a condition that can be enhanced by the provision of supports rather than as a more static disability.

Chapter 3

Moderate to severe cognitive impairment

Introduction

This chapter mainly uses the term 'moderate to severe cognitive impairment' unless discussing definitions which specifically use alternatives. Where comments or research applies specifically to only *moderate* cognitive impairment or *severe* cognitive impairment, this is made clear.

I explain definitions of moderate and severe cognitive impairment, prevalence, causal factors and identification and assessment. Regarding provision, I examine: curriculum, including cross-curricular links, and assessment; pedagogy; resources; therapy; and organisation. Within pedagogy, the chapter considers visual inputs, communication, developing autonomy and independence, and community-based vocational instruction.

Terminology and definitions

This chapter concerns children with 'moderate to severe cognitive impairment'. In the United States of America the term 'moderate to severe mental retardation' is often used. England currently uses the expression 'severe learning difficulties'. In some other countries, for example, Canada, Australia and Malta, the term 'moderate to severe intellectual disability' is preferred. Terminology as reflected in the names of organisations is changing in some countries. For example, the former American Association of Mental Retardation is now the American Association of Cognitive and Developmental Disabilities (www.aaidd.org).

The reason for conflating terms which in some countries are different (severe and moderate mental retardation) is that the implications of provision are similar. This is reflected in the term 'severe learning difficulties' which is used in England. In this English use of terminology, intelligence and functional respects are very similar to 'moderate to severe cognitive impairment/mental retardation' used elsewhere.

In the case of mild cognitive impairment there is contention about definition, assessment and provision. With regard to profound cognitive impairment (as we shall see in a later chapter), definition, assessment and provision are more widely agreed. Moderate and severe cognitive impairment comes between these two positions. It may be considered in relation to mild cognitive impairment and profound cognitive impairment.

Definition, assessment and provision are more clearly understood than is the case for mild cognitive impairment, but not as clearly as for profound cognitive impairment. While there is considerable agreement, there is still a certain amount of debate about the most suitable provision for children with moderate to severe cognitive impairment. This makes on-going monitoring of progress and development essential.

Moderate to severe cognitive impairment is defined in terms of a combination of intelligence levels and functional assessments. The *Diagnostic and Statistical Manual of Mental Disorders Fourth Edition Text Revision (DSM-IV-TR)* (American Psychiatric Association, 2000, p. 42) relates 'moderate retardation' to intelligence quotient (IQ) levels of 35/40 to 50/55. 'Severe retardation' is associated with IQ levels of 20/25 to 35/40. Consequently, the range for moderate to severe cognitive impairment is of IQ levels from 20/25 to 50/55. These ranges are treated with care – an IQ is not the sole criterion.

The diagnostic criteria for mental retardation in general also includes 'co current deficits or impairments in present adaptive functioning … in at least two of the following areas: communication, self care, home living, social/interpersonal skills, use of community resources, self-direction, functional academic skills, work, leisure, health and safety' (American Psychiatric Association, 2000, p. 49).

Definitions and descriptions also suggest the sort of provision from which children and young people concerned are found to benefit. The *Diagnostic and Statistical Manual of Mental Disorders* states that most people with *moderate* mental retardation acquire communication skills in early childhood. With some supervision, they 'can attend to their personal care' (American Psychiatric Association, 2000, p. 43). They can benefit from training in social and occupational skills. However, they are 'unlikely to progress beyond second-grade level in academic subjects' (ibid. p. 43).

Individuals with *severe* mental retardation tend to acquire little or no communicative speech in early childhood. Nevertheless, during the school age period they may learn to talk and can learn 'elementary self care skills'. They profit to a limited degree from teaching in 'pre-academic subjects' such as 'simple counting'. Individuals with severe mental retardation can also master skills such as sight-reading of some survival words (ibid. p. 43).

In England, 'severe learning difficulties' by convention broadly corresponds in IQ terms to the American 'moderate mental retardation' and 'severe mental retardation', that is an IQ range of 20/25 to 50/55 (Kushlick and Blunden, 1974). Guidance published by the government Department for Education and Skills (Department for Education and Skills, 2005, p. 6) (www.education.gov.uk) states that pupils with severe learning difficulties have 'significant intellectual cognitive impairments'. It continues:

> This has a major effect on their ability to participate in the school curriculum without support. They may also have difficulties with mobility and co-ordination, communication and perception and the acquisition of self help skills. Pupils with severe learning difficulties need support in all areas of the curriculum. Some pupils may use signs and symbols but most will be able to hold simple conversations (ibid.).

Their attainments will be within the upper 'P scale' range for much of their school careers. P scales are 'performance scales' (Qualifications and Curriculum Authority, 2001a, 2001b, 2001c). If a child is within the P scale range, this indicates attainments are 'below level 1 of the National Curriculum' (Department for Education and Skills, 2005, pp. 3–4). The description indicates that pupils with severe learning difficulties will for most of their schooling be working below a level usually entered by a typically developing child at about the age of 5 to 6 years.

Lower IQ levels are associated with greater possibility of the child having a medical background condition. Only around 40 per cent of individuals with an IQ level of 70 have such a condition. However, when individuals have an IQ below 50, 80 per cent have a medical background condition (Gillberg and Soderstrom, 2003).

In considering this guidance about likely abilities and skills, remember that the diagnostic criteria are broad generalisations. They are not intended to dampen realistic aspirations about what an individual child might achieve.

Prevalence

Given the flexibly applied nature of definitions, prevalence is not easy to establish. In the United States of America, it is estimated that of the population with mental retardation (mild, moderate, severe, profound), the group having moderate mental retardation constitute around 10 per cent. The group having severe mental retardation make up approximately

3 to 4 per cent. Mild mental retardation accounts for around 85 per cent and profound mental retardation for about 1 to 2 per cent (American Psychiatric Association, 2000, p. 43).

Consequently, the group with which we are concerned, those having moderate to severe cognitive impairment, constitute about 13 to 14 per cent of the population of those having cognitive impairment.

Causal factors

Classifications of mental retardation used in research tend to adopt severity criteria, such as the IQ range discussed earlier, or aetiology as touched on below (Hodapp and Dykens, 1994).

The *DSM-IV-TR* (American Psychiatric Association, 2000) considers predisposing factors for mental retardation in terms of various elements. These include:

- heredity;
- early alterations of embryonic development;
- pregnancy and perinatal problems; and
- general medical conditions acquired in infancy or childhood (ibid. pp. 45-6).

Examples of heritable conditions are Tay-Sachs disease, tuberous sclerosis, translocation Down syndrome and Fragile X syndrome.

Early alterations of embryonic development include chromosomal changes such as Down syndrome due to trisomy; or prenatal changes owing to toxins, such as maternal alcohol consumption, or to infection.

Among pregnancy and perinatal problems are foetal malnutrition, prematurity, hypoxia, infections, including viral infections, and trauma.

General medical conditions acquired in infancy or childhood include infections, trauma or poisoning, for example lead poisoning (ibid. pp. 45-6, paraphrased).

Estimates have been made of the percentages of cognitive impairment attributable to different broad causal factors:

- about 15 per cent was attributed to events occurring at conception;
- about 47 per cent was attributed to events after conception;
- about 12 per cent was attributed to non-biological causes;
- about 26 to 30 per cent had unknown causal factors (Crocker, 1992).

Among events occurring at conception are abnormalities of chromosomes as in Down syndrome (10 per cent) or genes as in phenylketonuria

(5 per cent). Events after conception may be prenatal (32 per cent), perinatal (11 per cent) and post natal (4 per cent). Non-biological causes include deprivation (Crocker, 1992).

For further information on causal factors covering chromosomal and genetic, and non-genetic biological factors (prenatal, perinatal and postnatal), see Baroff 1999, pp. 95–201. In the present text, the chapter on 'Conditions and factors associated with cognitive impairment' considers Down syndrome, Fragile X syndrome and other conditions mentioned above.

Identification and assessment

When considering definitions of moderate to severe cognitive impairment, we saw that this was defined in terms of intelligence level (as shown by an intelligence quotient) and a description of functional behaviour. It follows that identification and assessment draw on similar sources.

A judgement that a child has cognitive impairment is influenced by looking at two areas:

- intellectual functioning and
- adaptive behaviour/adaptive functioning (Algozzine and Ysseldyke, 2006, p. 17).

These can be examined using criteria in diagnostic frameworks, through commercial assessments, through curriculum-based assessment, and through observations in different settings such as home and school.

Criteria such as those described in relation to the *Diagnostic and Statistical Manual of Mental Disorders* (American Psychiatric Association, 2000, p. 42) inform the identification and assessment of moderate to severe cognitive impairment. You will recall that the diagnostic criteria for mental retardation include 'co current deficits or impairments in present adaptive functioning' in at least two of 'communication, self care, home living, social/interpersonal skills, use of community resources, self-direction, functional academic skills, work, leisure, health and safety' (p. 49).

Commercial assessments are also used. These include intelligence tests. The child's performance of sub tests of intelligence scales is carefully analysed. The *Wechsler Intelligence Scale for Children – Fourth Edition (WISC-IV)* (Wechsler, 2003) is standardised in various countries for children aged 6 to 16 years. It has sub tests for verbal comprehension, perceptual reasoning, working memory and processing speed. Commercial assessments of adaptive functioning are also used which set out a profile of strengths and weaknesses. These may relate to personal and social skills and may be called 'adaptive behaviour scales'.

In a similar way, assessments relating to educational provision include determining areas of relative strength and weakness. Assessments of adaptive behaviour may involve evaluations by parents, teachers and others familiar with the child's response to the demands of home, school, community and work.

Adaptive behaviours may be considered in three areas:

- daily living skills such as getting dressed;
- communication skills; and
- social skills, such as positive interactions with others (Algozzine and Ysseldyke, 2006, p. 17).

The American Association of Mental Deficiency suggested the following skill areas:

- communication
- community living
- employment
- functional academics
- health and safety
- home living
- leisure
- self-care and advocacy
- social skills (for a summary, see Algozzine and Ysseldyke, 2006, pp. 21–3).

Expectations of the level and range of adaptive behaviours vary according to the child's age. For example, vocational and social responsibilities take on particular meaning in later adolescence.

Provision

Provision needs to be continuously reviewed. The following sections look at approaches suitable for moderate to severe cognitive impairment. Where the cognitive impairment is on the borderline of moderate, you may wish to consider some of the approaches suggested with regard to 'mild cognitive impairment' in the earlier chapter. Where the child's cognitive impairment is very severe on the borderline of profound, you may wish to look at some of the approaches outlined for profound cognitive impairment in the subsequent chapter.

This is one reason why provision is kept under review, to ensure the child or young person is making good progress and developing well and questioning the provision where achievement is not as high as expected.

I consider the curriculum in relation to working at earlier age levels and building on familiar, practical experiences; and with regard to cross-curricular planning and work. I examine suitable approaches to assessment. Turning to pedagogy, I focus on visual inputs, communication, developing autonomy and independence, and community-based vocational instruction. The chapter also looks at the use of resources and at therapy.

Curriculum

Several aspects of the curriculum deserve particular mention. These are the importance of working at earlier age levels; building of well-known and practical experiences; and using cross-curricular links fully.

Working at earlier age levels

The curriculum for pupils with profound cognitive impairment is informed by very early infant development. That for children with moderate to severe cognitive impairment builds on this foundation. It moves more securely into areas of the curriculum and activities with a more recognisable subject basis. The term 'functional academic content' (Wehmeyer with Sands, Knowlton and Kozleski, 2002, pp. 190–203) is sometimes used. This helps convey the need for practicality and relevance.

Given the levels of attainment associated with moderate to severe cognitive impairment, it is important that the curriculum is broad and relevant. It must also provide flexibility for children to work on areas of the curriculum at levels typical of much younger pupils. At the same time, every effort is made to ensure the activities are chronologically age appropriate. Developing such a curriculum takes considerable thought and skill on the part of teachers and others. The activities aim to be engaging and suitable for the students' interests, but they also need to cover knowledge, skills and understanding that are usually acquired at an earlier age.

Small steps in the development of knowledge and skills in the curriculum will be reflected in schemes of work.

Building on familiar, practical experiences

When building up, adapting and refining schemes of work, curriculum developers use familiar activities before progressing to the less familiar. Among particularly important elements are:

- communication
- literacy

- numeracy and
- personal and social development, and community and leisure skills.

Each of these draws on the familiar and the practical.

Communication will focus on direct, relevant activities. More is said about communication in the later section on pedagogy. So far as the curriculum is concerned, communication activities need to be practically orientated and have real-life applications. Some students may use manual signing to help their communication.

Literacy may involve functional reading and functional writing. The student can learn to recognise common signs such as 'toilet' or 'washroom'. He can make use of business names he knows to find a shop or café. Learning to use a menu in a café or restaurant is a useful if difficult skill. Newspaper extracts can be consulted. Practical and relevant activities may include reading a street map of the local area, finding required sections labelled by names in the library, or categorising a compact disc music collection.

Functional writing can include daily writing activities. The student might keep a diary, make a list of items to be bought from a shop, or note down tasks to be accomplished during the day. He might take down a telephone message, write a note or letter, send an email, or prepare part of a school or community newsletter (see also Algozzine and Ysseldyke, 2006, pp. 38–41).

Numeracy and functional mathematics may involve day-to-day tasks. These include budgeting and using money, laying a table and sharing several items among a group. They can involve telling the time, writing and following a weekly schedule, and reading transport timetables. Yet other activities are reading energy meters and measuring areas for practical activities such as gardening (see also Algozzine and Ysseldyke, 2006, pp. 38–42).

Personal and social education brings in developing a sense of self, self-awareness, self-esteem and self-knowledge. Another way of considering the content of personal independence programmes is in terms of self-care, home management and community skills. Self-care skills are those such as washing and bathing, hair care, oral hygiene, feminine hygiene, toileting, dressing, eating and drinking and knowing one's belongings and keeping them safe. Sex and relationships education is likely to involve the specific teaching of some aspects that typically developing peers might learn incidentally, such as what 'private' means. Home management skills might concern selecting a menu, cooking and house cleaning.

Community skills encompass using local transport, knowing and responding to social sight vocabulary, shopping, choosing and pursuing hobbies, using community facilities and making choices and decisions. Understanding the roles of people who live in the local community might begin with those who work in the school (teachers, therapists, secretary, maintenance workers) and those who visit it (parents, people from other schools). It will include those at home (parents, siblings) and those who visit home (relatives, newspaper delivery, postal worker).

Opportunities and activities planned into the curriculum might include opportunities to show visitors around, coping with changes in anticipated routine such as going out for lunch when expecting to eat in school, and taking turns in a recess activity or game.

Leisure skills can be taught, encouraged and supported. The rules of sports and games are important, such as turn taking, working in a team and the specific rules of activities. Also the student may be helped to be more aware of opportunities for different activities at school, at home and in the community. The student can also learn to arrange to get to a leisure venue on time, and when to leave the venue to get home.

The common theme here is that practical, life-relevant activities are used wherever possible. The curriculum should be a rich source of such activities supplemented by any necessary resources. Often the necessary resources will emerge in the real-life setting. You do not need a play shop with plastic fruit if you go to a real fruit seller.

Cross-curricular links

To some extent the curriculum is developed using the notion of subject and curriculum areas such as communication, literacy, personal development and so on. These are not treated as water-tight compartments. Indeed, the real-life nature of the curriculum will help ensure learning takes place across several curriculum areas. Cross-curricular links are a planned and more formal way of ensuring areas of the curriculum relate to one another well. Such links between subjects and areas of the curriculum reinforce subject understanding and skills.

Skills and understanding associated with mathematics can be tracked into the schemes of work for other subjects and areas. Obvious examples are science, physical education, history, geography/environmental studies and technology. The use of practical, relevant activities helps ensure the application of mathematical skills. However, the contribution of other subjects is important in giving further opportunities to apply and develop these skills.

Teachers will recognise when a mathematical skill such as telling the time and measuring duration is involved in what they are proposing to teach. You will highlight this in planning. In physical education the student may be asked to take a turn at timing a partner carrying out a fitness circuit. You cannot assume that, even if the mathematical aspect has already been taught, the student will remember it or successfully transfer it to the new context.

You will remember that the practical demands of the new task might make it harder for the pupil to apply any knowledge they may have. Such links aim to help the pupil generalise skills and transfer knowledge to different situations. At first this is done in a guided and structured way to help reinforce and develop understanding.

Assessment

To make sure pupils' progress is recognised and celebrated, it is necessary to have small steps in assessment, perhaps with intermediate targets. You should ensure that you carry out assessments of understanding and skills across different situations, at different times and with different people. This is related to cross-curricular planning.

Regarding communication, you and others will need to engage with the pupil in a way and at a level he understands and to which he can respond. This provides opportunities to recognise and record the pupil's progress using communication strategies:

- in different areas of the curriculum (music, mathematics);
- with different people (various adults, other pupils, visitors, people in the community in visits to shops, cafés and on walks); or
- in different circumstances (with one person, with several people, with familiar people and with strangers).

In mathematics, a skill in counting to five can be applied when buying items in a shop, laying a table or setting out chairs for others. This provides good opportunities for assessing the application of skills in a social context. Particularly where skills are just developing, evidence of such applications represents progress in beginning to generalise knowledge gained and the skills acquired.

Many countries use curriculum-related assessments and/or standardised assessment of various aspects of attainment and development. In England, curriculum-related assessments are available to recognise progress below level 1 of the National Curriculum: the so-called 'P' scales (performance scales) (Qualifications and Curriculum Authority, 2001a, 2001b, 2001c). Commercially available packages may be used for more detailed assessments.

Portfolios of achievements are also used to give a wide-ranging celebratory indication of achievements. These portfolios of achievements are developed gradually over time with the fullest involvement of the pupil. They can apply to work in school and elsewhere, including providing evidence of leisure pursuits.

Setting of individual learning targets is related to assessment. An example is the use of Individual Education Programmes/Plans. It is important to involve the pupils in this process.

You might discuss targets for learning with the pupil and what might be the best ways of achieving them.

Pedagogy

Several aspects of pedagogy are especially important for pupils with moderate to severe cognitive impairment. These are:

- visual information;
- communication (general approaches and specific strategies; augmentative and alternative communication);
- developing autonomy and independence; and
- community-based vocational instruction.

Visual information

Presenting information visually to a child has such an obvious advantage over some other forms that it can be overlooked. It is the fact that normally the visual impression remains constantly available. This is so, for example, in the case of a symbol (although less so for manual signing). By contrast auditory information tends to be briefly accessible to the child. There are exceptions to this as when auditory information is deliberately repeated, as when a request is made several times. But generally, visual information is constantly available so long as the individual is observing, while other forms of information are not constantly apparent.

Regarding literacy, sight recognition approaches tend to be preferred to phonological ones. This is especially so where the pupil has certain difficulties. These difficulties are:

- poor phonological awareness (that is difficulties with an awareness that relates speech sounds to changes in meaning);
- problems with auditory memory; and
- hearing impairment.

Sight recognition methods may include the use of graphical symbols. These are described later in the section on 'communication'.

A pupil may have poor auditory memory. If so, in mathematics, he will tend to find difficulty where the teacher uses oral methods of teaching numeracy, including mental arithmetic. He is likely to prefer visual approaches especially where real-life contexts are used promoting problem solving. Reviewing strategies for teaching mathematics, Butler and colleagues (2001) found that for students with 'moderate mental retardation', predominant approaches involved structured direct instruction.

Where pupils with moderate to severe cognitive impairment do not have visual impairments, provision may capitalise on visual input. I have already alluded to the importance of visual input where a child has problems with phonological processing, auditory memory or hearing. I linked this with the use of sight recognition approaches to literacy and visual methods of teaching numeracy. Using visual symbols and whole word approaches for teaching and learning literacy also capitalises on visual input.

A child with Down syndrome may experience difficulty with short-term auditory memory. If so, an icon or pictogram can help the child make a connection enabling him to link letter sounds to letter names. Also, teaching reading may help reinforce and encourage language skills (Alton, 2001). You can take note of the student's responses of signing, vocalisation or verbal approximations. The student may have particular difficulties making phoneme-grapheme correspondences (linking sounds and written marks). If so, whole-word approaches may be more accessible. These approaches can use the possibly stronger visual skills of pupils by linking the sight of the whole word with the spoken response.

You can help guide visual discrimination by using strategies to improve a student's success in visual discrimination tasks. Training begins with an item (say a blue item) and eight identical distracters (say red items). The task is to match the key item with one provided (in this case an identical blue item). The number of distracters is gradually reduced so the pupil has a choice of only two items from which to choose the correct match (MacKay, 2002).

It will be seen that this strategy can be adapted to teaching in many areas of the curriculum. For example, the provided item might be a coin of a particular value, say a high value coin such as an American dollar or an English pound. The key item would be an identical coin. The distracter items would be other coins of smaller values, perhaps all American cents or all English pence. The gradual removal of the distracters leaving only two coins from which to discriminate will help the student recognise and discriminate higher value coins when using money.

When you use such skills-based approaches it is important you supplement them by opportunities to put the learning (i.e. discrimination) to practical use. In the coins example the student might be encouraged to select and use the higher value coin when buying an item in a shop once the correct coin can be reliably identified.

You may use and teach manual signing with students. The visual aspects of this are important. Also, signing programmes enable the adult to correct and refine communication because it is visual and three dimensional. Of course, such signing systems can also encourage verbal communication.

Communication

Communication is important for many reasons. It can help ensure the student is involved in their own learning. It opens up greater opportunities to express choices and to become more independent. In this section, I consider:

- general approaches to communication then particular strategies; and
- augmentative and alternative communication.

General approaches and specific strategies

Difficulties in speech and language include limitations in the expressive communication skills of children with severe cognitive impairment (Mar and Sall, 1999). It is important that the school setting encourages the child to communicate. Daily structure might include a brief arrival greeting session, and snack times and recess activities where communication with other pupils is encouraged. There may be regular group activities and paired activities. Additionally, you can make use of on-going opportunities to encourage and respond to pupils' communication and to make use of situations in which communication is necessary and valued.

Among specific strategies is the behaviour chain interruption strategy, which is used in already established contexts and routines. In this approach, a stream of well-established behaviour is interrupted so that the pupil is required to adopt new types of communication (Carter and Grunsell, 2001). The pupil may be preparing a snack such as toast. Previously the teacher has always laid out the bread on a plate for the pupil to put into an automatic toaster. This has become a well-established procedure.

A behaviour interruption strategy might involve starting snack time with the bread in a container. This requires the pupil to request the bread. At first it may be necessary to guide him towards the bread. The motivation for communication is the momentum of the routine task and the expectation that it will be completed. Also the tangible reward of the food is likely to act as a further incentive.

You will need to use professional judgement and skill. The aim is that the behaviour interruption strategy acts as an incentive to the child's communication. Unless you are careful with the structure and timing of the activity and its components it can become a frustration and a trigger for inappropriate behaviour. This suggests several principles:

- the strategy is not over used;
- the required communication is within the child's capacity;
- the approach is used to trigger not to teach the communication; and
- the child is rewarded (for example by praise) for communicating.

Augmentative and alternative communication

Augmentative and alternative communication uses single or combined approaches, according to a pupil's skills and preferences, to enable communication. The skills necessary for developing competence in communication have been described as:

- linguistic skills such as learning what pictures and symbols mean and combining symbols to make sentences;
- learning the technical skills required to operate the communication system, such as the layout of symbols;
- developing the knowledge and skills in social rules of interaction; and
- developing skills to communicate effectively beyond the limits of competence in augmentative and alternative communication (Light, 1989).

Approaches in augmentative and alternative communication include the use of signing, photographs and speech synthesisers. Other examples, discussed below, are objects of reference and symbols.

An *object of reference* is used to indicate an event or activity that may not be happening in the present. It might be used to help the student remember something that has happened or something that it is planned will happen later. It is also used when the pupil wishes to indicate a choice or decision. The object of reference is not the actual object or event, but is symbolic of the object or event. Objects of reference can be used to indicate a proposed activity or signal a proposed change of activity. They can help the pupil anticipate a task, or enable him to make a choice/decide an activity.

Visual *symbols* capitalise on visual input and are often used in connection with computer technology. Symbols are used to support emerging literacy (King-de Baun, 1990). They can be employed in a way that relates to language sequencing skills as pupils select and place the symbols in order, and for reading and writing.

So-called talking mats are used to supplement alternative and augmentative communication (www.talkingmats.com). These are not mats that produce synthesised sound when touched – the idea is much simpler than this. A textured mat such as a household mat is used on which various card symbols can be attached. Three sets of symbols covering 'issues', 'emotions' and 'influences' are used which the pupil can indicate in various ways. If he has a physical impairment, he might use eye pointing. The innovative and flexible use of these symbols enables quite extensive communication.

A smiling face and a frowning face can be attached to different halves of the mat and beneath them can be sorted things and experiences the student likes and dislikes. Or a task can be represented such as using a computer and the student can indicate what they find helpful and unhelpful in learning computing by indicating symbols that are grouped according to this criterion.

Developing autonomy and independence

Developing autonomy and independence is centrally important for all students. It allows the individual to use his own initiative to learn and gather information in his own time. For pupils with cognitive impairment it is also vital to encourage this ability. The development of autonomy and independence builds on aspects of provision such as having security and routine. Choice is the other side of the coin to routine. Choice offers the security of predictability and regularity; routine gives the opportunity for variety and exploration. Routines might include morning greetings, snack times, end-of-day farewells, personal care routines and more complicated ones such as preparing for a school trip.

Encouraging choice and decision-making contributes to developing autonomy and independence. You can review each lesson or activity plan to see if it presents opportunities for offering choices. This might include choice of drink and food, leisure activity, musical instrument, or whether to examine a fruit or vegetable in a science lesson. At first, there might be only two options, but this can be later extended. Initially, adult support may be necessary to enable the pupil to begin to make choices.

More complex decision-making can also be encouraged. You might ask one pupil which of the other pupils should be requested to carry out a task – for example taking a message. You can then ask why that particular pupil was chosen. When required to complete three activities, pupils can be asked to decide in which order he will carry them out and why. Reasons might be that it is the student's personal preference that the order makes it easier, that a favourite task is first (or last).

One way you can optimise a pupil's choice and decision-making is to develop a matrix. This lists daily activities down the side. These might be a greeting session, numeracy, literacy, leisure activities or visit to the post office. The matrix sets opportunities for choice across the top. These could be 'chooses between one or more activities'; 'chooses between two or more items' and 'chooses a work partner'. The intersections indicate that opportunities are offered in the ways indicated.

In numeracy, the pupil might choose between two activities leading to the same learning outcome. This might be 'counting to five' either to plant seeds in five pots or to count cups to prepare drinks for five pupils. In leisure activities, the child might choose from several hobbies. On trips outside the school the pupil will choose items of clothing to wear. The same matrix can be used from time to time to record the range of choices offered and to record the progress the pupil is making in exercising choice. Parents may use a similar approach at home.

Children with cognitive impairment tend to have difficulties using strategies for remembering and monitoring their performance (Henry and Maclean, 2002). Examining several studies, Copeland and Hughes (2002) considered the effects of encouraging and guiding pupils' goal/target setting on performance. Visual cues were often used to remind pupils of their targets or to give a clear indication of progress. An important success factor was giving pupils information on the accuracy of their performance.

Practical applications will also be used:

- laying the lunch table using tablemats with outlines for setting out cutlery (matching);
- planting bulbs in the garden and spacing them well (measuring);
- reading a bus or subway timetable (grid data).

Related to these, you can build opportunities for problem solving into curriculum schemes. Examples are 'How will we know when to go and catch the subway train?' and 'How will we know how many bulbs to plant?' and 'How can we make sure we have enough table settings?'

Progression is built into the approach. You might start by offering in a structured situation limited choice from two items or activities. Later you might extend this to a wider choice. At a later stage, you might use

the method to enable pupils to use problem solving to develop autonomy. Throughout all this, communication is encouraged and developed
so that the child can make his wishes known.

Community-based vocational instruction

Community-based vocational instruction may take some time and effort
to arrange, but can be a very good aspect of provision. The *DSM-IV-TR*
(American Psychiatric Association, 2000, p. 44) suggests most people
with *moderate* mental retardation tend to be able to benefit from training
in social and occupational skills (p. 43). Individuals with *severe* mental
retardation tend to profit to a limited degree from teaching in 'pre-
academic subjects' like 'simple counting' and can learn skills such as
basic social sight-reading.

The chapter on 'Profound cognitive impairment' mentioned the
possibility of vocational instruction, including community-based vocational instruction. Similar arguments apply to pupils with moderate to
severe cognitive impairment. The study of vocational instruction by
McDonnell et al. (1993) indicated significant student gains. It concerned
high school students with 'moderate to profound mental retardation'.

The school can help the student develop work skills such as following
directions, punctuality, staying on task and completing assignments.
You can do this by directly teaching these and providing settings where
they are put into practice and encouraged (Algozzine and Ysseldyke, 2006,
pp. 49–50). The contribution to a student's self-esteem can be very high
if he is able to contribute to a work process. It is part of the understanding of normalisation that if possible a student will learn work-related
skills.

Resources

When considering resources with regard to students with cognitive
impairment, a key factor is gaining access to learning and the curriculum.
Technology is used to assist this. Regarding access technology, Day
(1995) has identified three kinds of access:

- physical
- supportive and
- cognitive.

Physical access concerns using technology to eliminate or limit the physical
barriers to learning. One example is a communication aid speech

synthesiser with a bank of words and the flexibility to create new words. Another possibility is a device such as a 'BIGmac' allowing brief phrases to be programmed into it enabling a pupil to participate and respond. Physical aids to using a computer such as a roller ball can allow a pupil to demonstrate and develop an understanding of mathematical concepts. These can involve matching and sorting objects. Using three-dimensional graphics, the student might manipulate shapes which he may not be able to handle physically.

Supportive access involves technology aiding a pupil in carrying out a task that is difficult for him. This might be using a word processor to help with presentation where handwriting skills are poor. Another example is using speech output devices such as speech synthesisers and speech recognition software to enable writing.

To allow *cognitive access*, technology is used to present the curriculum in ways that make it more accessible. Three ways have been suggested (Detheridge and Stevens, 2001, p. 164). The first is 'simplifying the writing process'. This can involve using an on-screen grid of words, or symbols, and phrases that pupils can transfer to their own text to assist the writing process. The second way is 'allowing pupils to explore ideas and try things out before committing themselves to the final outcome'. For this the student can use a word processor that allows redrafting and editing before deciding to print the final version. Finally, technology is used in 'presenting information in small quantities that can be easily assimilated'. This includes using talking books or CD-ROMs presenting manageable pieces of information. These are often enhanced with pictures, video clips, animation, spoken commentary or music, which can be very motivating and enjoyable.

Therapy

For pupils with cognitive impairment it is essential that a range of professionals work closely together with each other and with parents and the student. Several therapists may be involved with a student.

As necessary, therapy will be provided for areas of development such as physical development. This may involve the physical therapist and/or the occupational therapist. Speech and language therapy may be necessary to help phonological difficulties and other aspects of language development. Teachers and therapists need to liaise closely including when assessing pupils, planning interventions and implementing them.

The school should allocate curriculum time for this to be done successfully. A child might work at least some of the time individually with a speech-language pathologist. Alternatively, a consultancy or other approach might be used. In a consultancy approach, the speech-language pathologist would work closely with teachers and others in making assessments and interventions. An alternative is to have trained assistants to deliver parts of the agreed speech and language intervention. Of course combinations of these approaches can be used so long as the people involved work together closely and understand and respect each other's roles.

School and classroom organisation

The importance of visual information and of communication has been discussed earlier. For students to gain the fullest benefit, the classroom is organised so that the best use is made of pupils' senses of sight and hearing. Furniture arrangements can complement good classroom acoustics to help ensure pupils can hear as clearly as possible and minimise distracting noises.

Given the importance of visual input, it is particularly important that the classroom is arranged so that pupils can notice and respond to visual cues. This may need to be reassessed throughout a typical day as furniture is moved and different groupings are adopted for different activities. There will need to be space for storing and using a wide range of technology to support learning.

Practical activities and real-life experiences are crucial and the school building may be used for such activities. You may involve students in designing and developing a school garden and nature trail, working in the school office, delivering messages and similar tasks. The support of all school staff is necessary for this to work well. The whole school is likely to be involved in arranging learning outside the school in shops, offices, banks, cafés, markets, post offices and elsewhere. Public transport may be used for much of the time. Where it is important to make the best use of limited time or where a learning venue is some distance from the school, the school's own transport may be used. All this has timetabling and organisational implications.

Thinking points

Readers may wish to consider, with regard to a particular school:

- how effectively the curriculum provides an appropriate range of relevant learning opportunities on which progress is suitably determined;
- the degree to which classroom organisation including pupil grouping is suitable to ensure progress; and

- the extent to which the range of pedagogic approaches is effective and reflects the requirements of pupils.

Key texts

Algozzine, B. and Ysseldyke, E. (2006) *Teaching Students with Mental Retardation: A Practical Guide for Teachers* Thousand Oaks, CA, Corwin Press

This practically orientated book is underpinned by professional knowledge and related research findings. Chapters cover definitions, prevalence, causes, diagnosis, associated characteristics, teaching, trends and issues. Chapter 6 concerns, 'What Teachers Should Know About Teaching Students with Severe Disabilities'.

Carr, A. (2006) (2nd edition) *The Handbook of Child and Adolescent Clinical Psychology: A Contextual Approach* London, Routledge

This text is written mainly for postgraduate psychology students and those undergoing professional training in clinical psychology. The book includes a chapter, 'Intellectual, learning and communication disabilities', with a section on intellectual disability. This covers characteristics, epidemiology, clinical features, aetiology, assessment and differential diagnosis, and interventions.

Drew, C. J. and Hardman, M. L. (2006) (9th edition) *Intellectual Disabilities Across the Lifespan* Upper Saddle River, NJ, Prentice Hall

This well-established book examines the impact of intellectual disability on education, social and psychological issues from conception to old age.

Chapter 4

Profound cognitive impairment

Introduction

This chapter concerns children and young people with 'profound cognitive impairment'. In the United States of America the equivalent term is 'profound mental retardation', although 'cognitive impairment' is also used. In England, in recognition of the frequent accompanying disabilities and disorders, the commonly used term is 'profound and multiple learning difficulties'. Other alternatives to 'cognitive impairment' include 'mental handicap' which is preferred in Hong Kong and other parts of Asia and 'intellectual disability' which is used in Australia and New Zealand.

I consider definitions, prevalence, causal factors, identification and assessment, and provision. Regarding provision, the chapter looks at: curriculum and assessment; pedagogy; resources; therapy; and school and classroom organisation.

Definitions

'Profound mental retardation' is defined in the *Diagnostic and Statistical Manual of Mental Disorders Fourth Edition Text Revision (DSM-IV-TR)* (American Psychiatric Association, 2000, p. 42) according to two factors.

The first aspect concerns limitations in intellectual functioning. It is associated with an intelligence quotient (IQ) range of below 20 or 25. However, IQ levels are interpreted with care, not being the sole criterion. Most children with profound mental retardation have an 'identified neurological condition' that accounts for the condition (ibid. p. 44). In early childhood impairments of sensory neural function are evident.

The second criterion concerns adaptive behaviour. The diagnostic criteria for mental retardation also include co current deficits or impairments in present adaptive functioning in at least two of the following areas:

- communication
- self-care
- home living
- social/interpersonal skills
- use of community resources
- self-direction
- functional academic skills
- work
- leisure
- health and
- safety

(American Psychiatric Association, 2000, p. 49)

As part of the description and specification of criteria, *DSM-IV-TR* refers to possible development, including that in adulthood, and the sort of provision to encourage it. The commentary focuses on the environment, the relationship with the care giver, suitable training and level of supervision. It states:

Optimal development may occur in a highly structured environment with constant aid and supervision and an individualised relationship with a caregiver. Motor development and self-care and communication skills may improve if appropriate training is provided. Some can perform simple tasks in closely supervised and sheltered settings.

(American Psychiatric Association, 2000, p. 44)

It will be seen that the commentary in the *DSM-IV-TR* criteria (American Psychiatric Association, 2000) refers to levels of supervision and, by implication, levels of support. Some definitions seek to focus less on criteria and more on the support considered suitable. The American Association on Intellectual and Developmental Disabilities (AAIDD) takes such a view. In 2002, the AAIDD agreed a supports-based definition. Cognitive impairment was regarded not so much as a relatively static disability and more as a condition able to be enhanced by the provision of supports.

However, there are problems with such a definition as I discussed in the earlier chapter on 'Mild cognitive impairment'. Briefly, to make a fair allocation of support assumes some previous judgement of 'need', which in turn would refer to characteristics of the person requiring the support. Support is specified to avoid specifying difficulty, and presumably possible negative labelling, but justifying support requires reference to the original difficulty. Nevertheless, some observers take the view that the notion of support provision could supplement existing definitions of cognitive impairment and might indicate possible pedagogic approaches.

In England, a definition of profound and multiple learning difficulties is provided in government guidance. This states that, in addition to 'severe and complex learning needs', pupils have

> other significant difficulties, such as physical disabilities or a sensory impairment. Pupils require a high level of support, both for their learning needs and for their personal care. They are likely to need sensory stimulation and a curriculum broken down into very small steps. Some pupils communicate by gesture, eye pointing or symbols, others by very simple language ...
>
> (DfES, 2005, p. 7)

There is a mixture here of potentially a criterion-based definition and a supports-based definition. The guidance adds that, throughout their school careers, the attainments of these students are likely to remain in a range typified by the lowest levels of widely used 'performance scales' ('P scales').

The relevant levels (P1-4) begin with generic aspects of development such as that pupils 'encounter' and 'show emerging awareness' of activities and experiences and extend to emerging understanding relatable to areas such as mathematics and communication, for example that they are aware of cause and effect in familiar mathematical activities (Qualifications and Curriculum Authority, 2001a, 2001b, 2001c and later amendments).

Given that children with profound cognitive impairment have associated disabilities, other books in this series are relevant. These include those in *The Effective Teacher's Guide to Sensory and Physical Impairments: Sensory, Orthopaedic, Motor and Health Impairments, and Traumatic Brain Injury*. Relevant chapters are 'Visual impairment', 'Hearing impairment', 'Deafblindness' 'Orthopaedic impairment and motor disorders' and 'Health impairment'. You may wish to reflect on the extent to which approaches described there can be adapted taking into account the child's profound cognitive impairment.

Prevalence

Studies suggest agreement on the prevalence of profound cognitive impairment in Western Australia (Wellesley et al., 1992) and several European countries (for example, France) (Rumeau-Rouquette et al.,

1998). Prevalence rates in these studies range from 0.06 to 0.08 per cent. In the United States of America, it is estimated that, of the population with mental retardation (mild, moderate, severe, profound), the group having profound mental retardation constitute about 1 to 2 per cent (American Psychiatric Association, 2000, p. 43).

Prevalence rates do not vary as widely as some other conditions such as developmental coordination disorder or reading disorder. Indeed, it is widely accepted that profound cognitive impairment is in comparison easier to define and identify. Small variation is nevertheless evident.

Some of the variation may be explained if we take the *DSM-IV-TR* (American Psychiatric Association, 2000, p. 49) definition as an example. There is difficulty in being precise about the level of the 'co current deficits or impairments in present adaptive functioning' as required by criteria. Another reason for differing prevalence rates may be the variety of areas that can be considered relevant in the *DSM-IV-TR* criteria. These are 'communication, self care, home living, social/interpersonal skills, use of community resources, self-direction, functional academic skills, work, leisure, health and safety' (ibid. p. 49). Because the criteria specify that 'at least two' of these areas should show deficits or impairments, the definition and assessment can include a child with two such impaired areas or all of them.

Furthermore, definitions vary from country to country. The example from England compared with that of the American *DSM-IV-TR* indicates this variation. The definition in England tends to include sensory and physical disabilities that often accompany profound cognitive impairment as part of the definition. On the other hand, *DSM-IV-TR* appears to view such disabilities as less fundamental to the definition.

However, *DSM-IV-TR* does recognise that the greater the mental retardation, the greater the likelihood of other conditions occurring. These include neurological, neuromuscular, visual, auditory and cardio-vascular conditions. This increase in co–occurring conditions is especially so if the cognitive impairment is severe or profound (American Psychiatric Association, 2000, p. 46).

Causal and related factors

Almost all children with profound cognitive impairment have organic brain damage. During their childhood period, it is evident there are 'considerable impairments' in sensory motor functioning (American Psychiatric Association, 2000, p. 44). Many rare syndromes each account for a small percentage of instances of profound cognitive impairment.

As already indicated, *DSM-IV-TR* observes that the greater the cognitive impairment, and especially if it is severe or profound, the greater the co-existing likelihood of other conditions (American Psychiatric Association, 2000, p. 46). It is widely agreed that the vast majority of people with profound cognitive impairment are also multiply disabled (Arvio and Sillanpaa, 2003). Many causes of cognitive impairment may lead to different degrees of impairment. Because of this you may find it useful to consult the section on causal factors in the chapter, 'Moderate to severe cognitive impairment'.

Conditions that do not of themselves lead to profound cognitive impairment may be associated with it. An example is cerebral palsy, a physical impairment affecting movement and linked with damage to the developing brain. Cerebral palsy is associated with 20 to 30 per cent of instances of profound mental retardation (Evans and Ware, 1987; Wellesley et al., 1992).

Identification and assessment

The identification of profound cognitive impairment includes identifying profoundly impaired cognitive functioning and other significant difficulties. These difficulties include physical disabilities, sensory impairment or a severe medical condition. Just as definitions and related application of criteria may vary, so identification and assessment is not clear-cut. The validity of assessments and how they can be improved is a matter of debate.

Educational assessments determine areas of relative strengths and weaknesses using various assessments. Intelligence tests are carried out paying particular attention to analysing performance on sub scales. Developmental scales are judiciously used. In the use of such assessments, you and your colleagues will be concerned that the assessments are, among other things:

- valid
- useful and
- purposeful.

Valid assessments measure what they are designed to measure. Useful tests serve a clear purpose that benefits the child. Purposeful assessments can serve a variety of uses such as indicating approaches to instruction that may be effective.

In using assessments of adaptive functioning, testers also look for a profile of strengths and weaknesses. The *Vineland Adaptive Behaviour Scales* (Vineland II) (second edition) (Sparrow, Chicchetti and Balla, 2006) may be used to support the identification and assessment of children with cognitive impairment. It is designed as a measure of personal and social skills required for everyday living from birth to adulthood. Its scales cover the domains of communication, daily living skills, socialisation and motor skills. Information emerging from the scales is also used to inform educational and treatment planning and to track progress.

Assessment may take into account such developments as the 2002 AAIDD supports-based definition described earlier. If so, the provision of supports may be part of the assessment process. A more dynamic process of assessment might result that could also point the way to longer-term pedagogic and support strategies.

Provision

Provision is considered in relation to the curriculum and assessment, pedagogy, resources, therapy and care, and school and classroom organisation. As will be seen there is a distinctive profile of provision that is considered effective with students with profound cognitive impairment in encouraging their progress and development.

Curriculum

Children and young people with profound cognitive impairment function at a very early developmental level. Accordingly, the curriculum is informed by knowledge of typical early infant development. One working assumption is that the child may be developing in a similar way to a child without cognitive impairment, but at a slower speed. However, it is not assumed that in all instances a pupil with cognitive impairment will develop in the same way as a typically developing infant. Consequently, provision takes account of idiosyncratic development and the effects of other disabilities.

Planning ensures a rich variety of curriculum experiences and draws on what appear to be the pupils' developmental learning requirements. Crucial additional curriculum requirements such as therapy and special programmes are integrated into provision. Among special programmes may be one encouraging communication.

Priorities such as those expressed in an Individualised Education Programme/Individual Education Plan are likely to involve the acquisition of basic and fundamental skills. These skills may not necessarily fit into school curriculum subject categorisations. Given the impairments in adaptive functioning associated with mental retardation (American Psychiatric Association, 2000, p. 49), the curriculum will also ensure that practical, functional activities are planned in various areas. These will include: 'communication, self care, home living, social/inter-personal skills, use of community resources, self-direction, functional academic skills, work, leisure, health and safety' (ibid.).

Assessment

What should an assessment system suitable for students with profound cognitive impairment accomplish? Several functions or qualities have been suggested (Ouvry and Saunders, 2001). The assessments should be able to:

- record experiences as well as responses or achievements and pro-cesses additionally to outcomes;
- be completed by a range of staff;
- record achievement in subject-specific understanding and individual priorities;
- relate directly to each pupil's Individual Education Plan;
- accommodate a wide variety of pupil responses to a situation;
- record responses in whole class, small group and individual sessions (ibid. p. 253, paraphrased).

The progress of pupils with profound cognitive impairment might be idiosyncratic. This progress might not necessarily conform to assump-tions of hierarchical child development underpinning assessments of vertical progression. Therefore, assessment will include recognition of the breadth of a pupil's experiences. These can be the opportunities students have had to develop a skill or knowledge in different ways, and the technological or adult support necessary to achieve a particular outcome. It will include the assessment of understanding and skills across different situations, at different times and with different people.

Many countries use curriculum-related assessments, standardised assessments of various aspects of attainment and development, and portfolios of achievement. In England, curriculum-related assessments, so-called 'P' scales (performance scales), recognise progress below level 1 of the National Curriculum. National Curriculum level 1 is usually reached by a typically developing child at about the age of 5 to 6 years (Qualifications and Curriculum Authority, 2001a, 2001b, 2001c and later amendments). More detailed commercially available teacher-completed assessments are also used.

Related to curriculum-based assessments is task analysis. This allows detailed assessments to be made of a task or activity and enables educa-tors to identify aspects requiring further instruction (Bigge, Best and Heller, 2001, pp. 121–48). Task analysis emerged from behavioural perspectives. However, the flexibility of the method has led to it being used by teachers and others influenced by other approaches, including cognitive ones. Task analysis may be applied in various ways. It can relate to tasks seen as a prerequisite to other ones, such as picking up an item before using it. Task analysis can relate to tasks logically linked as part of a procedure such as dressing oneself.

Task analysis typically involves:

- deciding the aims and objectives for teaching and learning;
- determining and specifying the desired learning outcome;
- specifying in detail the tasks and elements of tasks the pupil will be carrying out;
- prioritising and sequencing the tasks;
- agreeing suitable ways of teaching and learning likely to lead to the desired learning outcomes;
- deciding the support needed and the optimum learning environment; and
- setting up ways of assessing the pupil's progress and achievement and evaluating the whole process.

When you record the results of assessments this enables you to determine a starting point for a proposed intervention and allows you to monitor progress. You make a baseline assessment. Using this baseline you set a target. The aim is to reach the target through a particular pedagogic approach, or extra time being allocated or some other strategy. After a specified time you make a further assessment to indicate progress from the baseline and also to give an indication of the success or otherwise of the intervention.

It is important to make a note of any developments that take place over the same period of time. This includes things the pupil has not been observed to do before or some skill the pupil appears to have transferred to a new situation. A child may have used a manual sign in the classroom to request a 'drink' when the environment supports this, as when daily routine preparations are being made for snack time. After a while, he may be observed making the sign in a different context, such as the play areas. You may note him making the sign at a different time, such as when he first arrives at school. This would be recorded. Even more importantly you and others would respond to the sign!

Pedagogy

Central to suitable pedagogy for students with profound cognitive impairment are:

- developing communication;
- task analytic instruction;
- multi-sensory approaches and daily living experiences; and
- community-based vocational instruction.

Communication

The diagnostic criteria in *DSM-IV-TR* (American Psychiatric Association, 2000, p. 49) for mental retardation refers to 'co current deficits or impairments in present adaptive functioning' in a least two areas. These include communication and social/interpersonal skills. The importance of supporting the communication of students with profound cognitive impairment is vital.

When working with students with profound cognitive impairment, you need to be careful when interpreting apparent signs. As part of this awareness, those working with the student need to check constantly that their responses seem suitable in the student's terms. In other words, is the student reacting in a way that would make sense if they were interpreting your actions in the way you intend them? This does not guarantee that the student is interpreting your responses and acting in the right way, but can be an indication.

Among behaviour having the potential to be communicative is physiologically related behaviour such as 'freezing' or being apparently startled. But temporary rigidity of the body or a limb can have different origins. It may indicate dislike or fear. It may be related to physical and motor impairment. Smiling or grimacing may respectively indicate pleasure or displeasure at something happening in the surroundings. Alternatively, it may be related to an inner state. Facial expressions may not invariably indicate what they are commonly thought to convey.

There are other aspects of non-verbal behaviour to which the teacher and others may seek to respond. Among these are: posture; withdrawal or approach responses; arm waving or other gestures. Further aspects are: pushing someone or something away; reaching for something and many other movements that may be indications of feeling, preference or some other communication. Turning towards a sound or showing apparent attention through fixing one's gaze or following a person or object with one's gaze are other potentially communicative indications.

But some behaviour may be ritualistic or obsessive and not relate to the present environment either internal or external in the usual way. Sounds may indicate feelings or preferences or other matters. These may be apparently contented sounds such as babbling or excited noises. They may be seemingly unhappy sounds such as shrieking or crying. Again, you need to be alert to their possible intended meaning and how you should respond.

Some early behaviours and responses may be spontaneous, but where an adult in turn responds to them, they can come to have communicative significance. Such consequences are of course part of the development of communication for all children (Pease, 2000, pp. 41–2). These patterns of response might take a long time to become routine and secure. Sensitivity on the part of the adult communicative partner to what the pupil does and how he reacts is essential. Pupil behaviours and responses can lead to the teacher or other adult responding in a way that lays the basis for the gesture or sound or glance to be invested with communicative intent. Sensitivity is also necessary if and when the pupil begins to point or gesture to ensure attempts to communicate are not missed.

'Intensive Interaction' is an approach using one-to-one sessions and seeking to 'help the person learn fundamentals of communication – eye contacts, facial expressions, turn taking' (Nind and Hewett, 2001, p. 17). It can involve encouraging interaction as it were for its own sake or can enable interaction with other children and help the pupil gain access to the curriculum through improving communication and inter-personal behaviour. The approach involves 'regular, frequent interactions between the practitioner … and the individual with learning disabilities, in which there is no task or outcome focus, but in which the primary concern is the quality of the interaction itself' (Hewett and Nind, 1998, p. 2). (The term 'learning disabilities' in the context just quoted appears to refer to cognitive impairment.)

Data were collected for a group of five children with 'profound and multiple learning difficulties' over a year. This was gathered during teacher-led group time (not directly aimed at developing communication) and in intensive interaction time. It was found that children demonstrated more consistent and advanced behaviour in the time given to intensive interaction (Watson and Fisher, 1997). Single child reports also suggest that daily intensive interaction sessions can develop communication, increase participation in positive social contact, and sometimes leads to reduced stereotyped behaviour (Nind and Kellett, 2002).

Some students with profound cognitive impairment may respond to and use symbolic communication. Objects of reference may be used where the object can be invested with meaning for the student. You need to take care the item that appears to be an object of reference (for example, a plate indicating meal time) is indeed acting in a symbolic capacity. Otherwise, the teacher may mistake an item that is simply a classically conditioned stimulus only associated with the reward of food, as an object of reference. The student may learn to use and understand visual symbols – for example conveying various activities or places. Or symbols such as a smiling face or angry face may be used to indicate preferences, choices and feelings.

Where a pupil can communicate by simple language, it is important that this too is encouraged and that adults and other pupils are ready to respond. The spoken language used by adults to a pupil does not have to be overloud, stilted and telegraphic. But neither should the pupil be swamped with streams of talk. Key words can be naturally stressed and repeated and accompanied by the item to which the speaker is referring. Manual sign language is used to communicate and to supplement verbal communication.

Also, where a child has profound cognitive impairment and is also deaf, manual signing and lip reading take on particular significance. If the child is blind, aural-oral communication and opportunities to develop close familiarity with surroundings come to the fore. Should the child with profound cognitive impairment also be deafblind, then training in the significance and importance of touch is central and hand-over-hand work (Hodges, 2000, p. 179) may be used for communication.

Where such symbolic communication is learned, it opens up the opportunity to communicate about items or people that may not be present or about proposed activities. (See the earlier chapter on 'Moderate to severe cognitive impairment' for further discussion.) In the present chapter, later sections on resources, organisation and challenging behaviour also provide further information on communication.

Task-analytic instruction

Task analysis has already been mentioned in relation to assessment (Bigge, Best and Heller, 2001, pp. 121–48). As well as it being a form of assessment, there are implications for intervention. This section considers how the approach can inform teaching and learning outlining an example of teaching a child to drink from a covered cup holding it in both hands.

The desired learning outcome is that the child, when thirsty and when a covered cup containing drink is placed on a tray in front of him, will pick up the cup and drink from it. The elements of the task are to look at the cup, to place both hands round it, to raise it to the mouth and tilt it so the contents can be drunk. The sequence of subtasks might be taught in the order just explained. Alternatively, they might be taught using so-called backward chaining where the child is helped or prompted for all but the final part of the sequence and encouraged to finish that, progressively being encouraged to complete earlier parts of the sequence without support.

A suitable way of teaching this might be through using physical prompts for each part of the sequence and gradually fading these out, or by using time delay. The support needed might be one adult the child knows well, and a quiet environment without distractions. The pupil's progress might be recorded in terms of the parts of the sequence. Where there is more rapid progress on certain occasions, the possible reasons might be noted so that they feed into the evaluation of what worked best and why.

Multi-sensory approaches and daily living experiences

Three ways of using a multi-sensory approach have been suggested:

- to stimulate the senses;
- to be part of meaningful activities; and
- to help access to subject-based activities (Ouvry and Saunders, 2001, p. 254).

A child may be less able to explore the environment without considerable support and encouragement. He may be less inclined to do so because of accompanying physical or motor difficulties. Stimulating the senses is a way of encouraging responsiveness in a child constrained by ability or inclination. Sensory stimulation is a way of introducing different experiences to the pupil and encouraging his interest and response. Senses are stimulated to develop perceptual skills to gain information from the environment.

To the extent that this approach uses specialised equipment with no inherent meaning in situations lacking meaningful context, it might provide a starting point for the functional use of sense. However, in this context, it has 'limitations as a long term teaching technique' (Ouvry and Saunders, 2001, p. 245).

A sensory stimulation room may be used. In such rooms, devices may be used that respond to touch or sound by producing sounds or visual effects. These may encourage responses from the student. There may be a soft room perhaps with a ball pool, a projector, bubble tubes, fibre optic lighting, and a transmitter of sound effects or music. As well as stimulating the senses and encouraging responses, the rooms can have other functions. They can create an environment with soothing sounds and soft lighting to help a child relax if he is frustrated or distressed.

Such assumed uses are sometimes rather taken for granted. Evaluation of any supposed benefits is important. Schools may wish to ensure they make the assumed educational and therapeutic effects of sensory rooms explicit in their policy development and planning. They may also wish to evaluate supposed educational gains rigorously. This will include a critical look at the likely meaningfulness of the experiences for the pupil, and the supposed personal impact.

The second way in which multi-sensory experiences can be used and developed is to incorporate sensory experiences into activities having their own 'structure and meaning', but that have been devised to give opportunities for sensory work. The sensory experiences are based on what are judged to be the priorities for the child. A priority might be attending to and visually tracking an object. However, these priorities will be incorporated in an activity such as drama. The activity could be handling then watching a glove puppet as part of a story.

The third way of using a multi-sensory approach is to enable participation in subject-related activities. These subjects, such as mathematics, science and history, have skills and understanding associated with them. Some aspects of these may be accessible to pupils with profound cognitive impairment. In a science topic on plant growth, the student may be encouraged to touch, smell, observe and perhaps taste a fruit at early and later stages of growth. These experiences might be reinforced by grouping paired examples of fruits that are 'small' and 'big'. A difficulty is that the topic may or may not have meaning. If the topic is outside the pupil's understanding, the sensory experiences may seem to the pupil fragmented and meaningless or may not convey what is intended.

The challenge for the teacher is to identify in teaching contexts opportunities to encourage sensory experiences for the pupil that aid further development. This might be progress from tolerating to attending, from attending to participating, or from participating to understanding. There are two main intentions. The first is that the pupil should be able to grasp meaning in the sensory experience itself. The second intention is developing an awareness of the meaning it has in the context of the activity. The broader aim is that as the pupil attends to these contextual meanings, he begins to develop increasing familiarity with them leading to potential further learning.

There is increasing consensus that the level of access afforded by multi-sensory approaches should not be regarded as sufficient in itself because such experiences do not necessarily have meaning for the pupil (Ouvry and Saunders, 2001, p. 245). Sensory experiences it is suggested should be extended to give opportunities for conceptual learning and to help the pupil understand better his surroundings, daily activities and everyday experiences (Carpenter, 1994).

There are a host of activities that can be stimulating to the senses and also have the potential to be meaningful. The student can prepare food (and eat it!), wash, take part in a game or leisure activity, visit a park or market, explore a nature trail, make music or shape pottery.

Community-based vocational instruction

The *DSM-IV-TR* (American Psychiatric Association, 2000, p. 44) suggests with regard to people with profound mental retardation that some 'can perform simple tasks in closely supervised and sheltered settings'. Baroff (1999, p. 59) maintains that an adult who is 'profoundly retarded' may ' ... be unable to perform any useful work, although with training in an activity center may achieve a work-activity level of productivity'. For older students, as part of transition from school to post-school settings, vocational instruction including community-based vocational instruction can have an important role.

Community-based instruction can have a positive impact on the development of adaptive behaviour of students. A study with 34 high school students with 'moderate to profound mental retardation' found that students made statistically significant gains in three of the four domains of the *Scales of Independent Behaviour* (McDonnell et al., 1993).

The coordination of all parties involved, including potential employers, school, rehabilitation counsellor, those making transport arrangements, volunteers, and those involved in other support services, help maximise the potential benefits of this provision. Planning for community-based vocational instruction takes account of local circumstances and job opportunities.

Training schedules are devised to help students develop the necessary skills for employability and employment. Task analyses may be made of the main tasks that the student will be expected to carry out. These might be cleaning procedures or packing skills. Such training helps students develop choices about what they would like to do – for example indicated by expressions of pleasure or dislike when carrying out tasks.

This also gives employers the opportunity to see what a student with profound cognitive impairment, perhaps with co-worker support, is able to do. Education supports suitable for students aged 18 to 21 have been outlined (Wehmeyer et al., 2002). These supports should be provided in an age-appropriate setting that allows social contact and encourages inclusion in the community. The services should be 'outcomes orientated'.

Remember that such training may be suitable for 'some' students. An individual judgement will have to be made about whether a student is able to respond to community-based vocational training. This will take account of safety, health, evidence the student understands and enjoys the activity and other matters. This can be reviewed from time to time to ensure that aspirations for students with profound cognitive impairment are as high as possible.

Resources

The use of resources for students with profound cognitive impairment is aimed among other things at encouraging communication and personal and social interaction, making choices, making fullest use of experiences outside the school.

Activities may be enhanced and structured using the visual and auditory capabilities of digital videodiscs (DVDs) or interactive compact discs. Also, technology is employed to aid communication and social interaction. Initially, these approaches may enable the child to become aware that his actions can affect others.

Making choices, as well as being an aspect of communication, contributes to greater autonomy. It may be taught using adult prompting and/or the use of a switch-activated reinforcer. Prompting may be used to teach switch activation and/or discrimination between different choices (Ware, 2005, p. 73). Case studies have indicated that multiple micro switches can be useful for enhancing different responses in children with profound disabilities. The wider range of response opportunities and the more differentiated input from the environment lead to higher levels of responding (Lancioni et al., 2002).

For any activity in school or an outside trip, a digital camera or video camera can be used to record events. Very soon after the activity is completed images can be transferred to computer and projected. The teacher and others will need to observe the student's responses to see if there is any indication that what is being shown conveys to the student anything about the activity recently carried out. Such images are a form of symbolic communication that the student may not recognise or understand.

For students able to use symbolic communication, computer technology allows the flexible use of many symbols. However, the teacher will need to ensure the pupil links the symbol to the intended object, activity or person. Dedicated communication devices may be used involving electronic communication systems speaking programmed messages when the pupil activates locations marked by symbols.

Computer-aided communication may involve a voice production device with a computer-based bank of words and sentences that can be produced by pressing the keyboard keys.

Therapy

As a teacher, you will need to understand the roles of a wide range of therapists and other professionals when working with students with profound cognitive impairment. You will need to share information effectively so that there is no unhelpful overlapping of roles and responsibilities. Equally, different professionals will need to make sure that nothing is left undone because one set of professionals thinks others are dealing with it. In a school, or in other services, this seamless service does not happen automatically. It requires time for planning and reflection as well as time to carry out face-to-face work with students. This relates to school organisation where the timetable for students and staff needs to be sensitive to these matters.

Physical and motor disability may be associated with conditions such as spina bifida, which may accompany profound cognitive impairment. These disabilities will require the support and advice of a physiotherapist, occupational therapist and others. The role of these professionals is to develop and oversee specific programmes encouraging suitable posture and optimum movement. Movement and exploring the environment contribute considerably to learning. Therefore, where these are impaired, it is vital to make the most of what mobility there is for pupils with profound cognitive impairment.

Medical conditions have their own implications both for care and in their effect on education and these are assessed for each child. Consider the example of cystic fibrosis. This is a life-threatening condition in which thick mucus is produced on the lungs and pancreas resulting in cysts. If a child with profound cognitive impairment has cystic fibrosis, he will require regular physiotherapy to clear his lungs. Another example is epilepsy. School staff may need to administer medication for seizures to a child with profound cognitive impairment who also has epilepsy.

School and classroom organisation

School and classroom organisation for students with profound cognitive impairment concerns:

- awareness of the student's behavioural state;
- developing a 'responsive environment'; and

- making the best use of classroom routines to aid learning and development.

An acute awareness of and an on-going assessment of the pupil's behaviour state underpins much of the organisation of the learning environment for pupils with profound cognitive impairment. Creating an environment responsive to pupils' signs of attention and other behaviour is clearly important. This importance is highlighted when one reflects on the fact that much of the time the student may be asleep or drowsy.

Students observed in research by Guess and colleagues (1990) were awake and alert only about half of their time in school. Such findings underscore the importance of teachers and others making continuing assessments of the behaviour state of each pupil. Doing this helps optimise opportunities for learning in the times when the pupil is more alert and responsive.

A range of strategies is brought together under the term 'responsive environment' (Ware, 2005). This approach is considered important in encouraging social, intellectual and communicative development. It is essentially the creation of an environment in which pupils with cognitive impairment 'get responses to their actions, get the opportunity to give responses to the actions of others, and have the opportunity to take the lead in interaction' (ibid. p. 1).

Greater awareness of a pupil's behaviour state is an aspect likely to improve the effectiveness of approaches such as 'room management'. This is used with groups of pupils and adults are assigned to one of three roles:

- individual helper
- group activity manager or
- mover (Lacey, 1991).

The individual helper tends to be involved with one pupil at a time on intensive work. She will vary the time spent with individuals from several minutes to longer periods depending on the pupil, the task and other factors. The group activity manager makes sure that the other pupils are occupied. Students might be experiencing a game or some other activity that is not focused intensively on skill building. The mover ensures the smooth running of the group. She deals with visitors, prepares materials or tidies away. The adult roles may be rotated about every hour.

While this approach increases the levels of adult attention for each pupil, it does not necessarily ensure that pupils are more engaged in the tasks (Evans and Ware, 1987). This suggests that the level of the pupil's engagement is monitored. The mover might do this if circumstances allow or if arrangements are made to make the job possible. The mover should be able to monitor effectively if there are few interruptions, preparation is done jointly before the sessions begin and there is not too much mess to tidy up. Factors that increase the pupil's engagement can then be noted and the approach gradually modified to ensure pupils are optimally engaged. These modifications will take account of the pupil, the task and the time of day, the aim being to get the best from room management while ensuring better pupil engagement.

It is important to create an environment that is sensitive to movements and sounds made by the pupil. This is in order that these environmental responses will in their turn bring about a response in the child. Pupils should be enabled to, through their actions, control aspects of their surroundings. Related to this is encouraging, perhaps initially with much support, choice and decision-making. Choices and decisions might involve food and drink, or leisure activity, whether to go out or stay in the classroom, and with whom to sit.

More specifically in creating an environment conducive to communication and development, establishing contingency awareness is very important. Contingency awareness involves the child being aware of the link between his behaviour and its consequences. Switch-operated reinforcers may be used. The child may be prompted to use the switch so that he will experience his action and its consequences repeatedly and link the two. What are the indications that a link is being made? Evidence is that the child is operating the switch more frequently (to receive the reinforcer) and his showing apparent pleasure in the activity.

School routines such as morning greetings, mealtimes and snack times and personal care procedures are used to extend pupils' understanding and skills by building on what is familiar to them. These can be linked to resources to develop understanding further. The resources themselves can come to acquire meaning by being associated with familiar activities. A particular cup regularly used for mealtimes at school may come to be associated with these times.

Routines can also invest several items with meaning in the sense that one item might indicate to the pupil that another may follow and this notion of sequence can contribute to the activity being imbued with greater meaning. The pupil might be shown a cooking utensil to indicate that a food preparation session is imminent. The pupil then sees the bread and a toaster and begins to link the two items to toast being made. Each item, the cooking utensil, the bread and the toaster, gains meaning and the activity begins to make sense as one associated with preparing food.

For students who may be able to understand symbolic communication, routines may be used to aid communication. The cup regularly used can signal that a snack or mealtime is imminent. That is the cup is used as an 'object of reference' for mealtimes. This gives the pupil an indication that there is about to be a change and what the change entails. Objects of reference can be developed in a similar way for regular classroom activities. Using a computer can be signalled by a compact disc. Food preparation may be heralded by a cooking utensil. A piece of swimming costume can be the indication that swimming/hydrotherapy is imminent.

Thinking points

Readers may wish to consider with reference to a particular school:

- the extent to which the curriculum and assessment fit closely together to ensure progress and development for the child;
- how communication and the responsiveness of the environment are optimised;
- how the school's organisation including pupil grouping and management enhances provision;
- how effectively arrangements for medical procedures and care are integrated into the school day.

Key texts

Aird, R. (2001) *The Education and Care of Children with Severe, Profound and Multiple Learning Difficulties* London, David Fulton Publishers

This book discusses both severe learning difficulties (moderate to severe cognitive impairment) and profound learning difficulties (profound cognitive impairment). The book covers a broad range of issues including ensuring the curriculum is sufficiently responsive to the learning and other 'needs' of the pupils as well as requirements for a broad curriculum.

Crone, D. A. and Horner, R. H. (2003) *Building Positive Behaviour Support Systems in Schools: Functional Behavioural Assessment* New York, Guilford Press

The book includes case examples of developing and using functional behavioural assessments within school systems. Appendices provide supportive charts and proformas.

Chapter 5

Conditions and factors associated with cognitive impairment

Introduction

Previous chapters have examined the broad ranges of cognitive impairment and the implications for the curriculum, assessment, pedagogy, resources, therapy, and school and classroom organisation. The present chapter looks at conditions and factors. There are a wide range of these. In describing some I give indications of the provision that may be required in addition to the general provision for cognitive impairment.

Many conditions are syndromes, so the chapter begins with an explanation of what a syndrome is with some examples. I then outline several syndromes relating to cognitive impairment, for example Down syndrome. After this, I describe other conditions that can be associated with cognitive impairment, for example Tay-Sachs disease. I next consider some factors that are associated with cognitive impairment including hypoxia and social and family circumstances. A section is included on challenging behaviour. Of course, not all children with cognitive impairment exhibit challenging behaviour, but where it occurs, there are particular approaches that can be helpful.

At the end of the chapter, readers are reminded of the requirements of education whether they are general to all children, individual to a specific child or common to a type of disability or disorder such as cognitive impairment. The contribution of knowledge about certain conditions and factors relating to cognitive impairment is seen in this context.

Syndromes: their definition, terminology and diagnosis

Definition of syndromes

A syndrome refers to a group of signs and/or symptoms. They occur together with enough regularity and predictability to be considered a pattern. This pattern is given an identifying name, for example Down syndrome. By classifying features in this way, predictions can be made about the likely outcomes for anyone identified as having the syndrome.

The naming of syndromes

There are a bewildering number of syndromes and they are named in a range of ways: after the person who identified the syndrome, after a physical aspect, after a certain type of characteristic behaviour or after the cause.

Syndromes are frequently named after the person who first identified them as in the case of Asperger syndrome, which is named after the paediatrician Hans Asperger who first described it. Autism is sometimes called Kanner syndrome after the American Leo Kanner who first outlined its symptoms. Tourette syndrome is named after the French neurologist Gilles de la Tourette and indeed it is sometimes given the full title of Gilles de la Tourette syndrome.

Others syndromes get their names from physical features that are especially noticeable. Among the characteristics of Menkes Kinky Hair syndrome is that normal hair becomes sparse and twisted. Cat-eye syndrome is associated with characteristic eyes.

Some syndromes are named according to certain behaviour. Cri du Chat syndrome is typified by the infant having a shrill cry rather like a kitten mewing. Pathological Demand Avoidance syndrome is associated with an avoidance of the regular demands of day-to-day life. The individual adopts strategies such as distracting adults, violence, excuses and seeming to become incapacitated.

The causes or apparent causes sometimes give the syndrome its name. Fragile X syndrome is so named because of the breakage of the tip of an X chromosome. Foetal Dilantin syndrome may be brought about when a mother who is epileptic takes the anti-convulsant drug Dilantin during pregnancy, affecting the foetus. This can lead to the child having growth deficiency, heart defects and cognitive impairment.

Alternative names for syndromes may draw on different sources. Cri du Chat syndrome, named after the distinctive infant cry, is also called Lejeune syndrome after the person who first identified it.

Diagnosing syndromes

When syndromes are diagnosed, it is important to remember that a minor abnormality occurring on its own does not specify a syndrome. Skin tags in front of the ear when found with a range of other characteristics can indicate Goldenhar syndrome. But skin tags on the ears alone can have many other causes and would not indicate Goldenhar syndrome.

Furthermore, a particular feature can occur in several syndromes. An abnormally small cranium (microcephaly) is associated with Williams syndrome (described later), Smith-Lemli-Opitz syndrome (a condition brought about by a defect in synthesising cholesterol and leading to many congenital anomalies) and other syndromes. An underdeveloped lower jaw is a feature of both Acrodysostosis syndrome (a rare congenital malformation syndrome) and Aarskog syndrome (an inherited condition affecting height, muscles, facial appearance and genitals).

As indicated earlier, a syndrome is identified according to a number of characteristics that tend to occur together. However, every abnormality that helps define a syndrome does not have to be present in every instance. In some syndromes the likelihood of the feature being present is specified in diagnostic criteria. In Congenital Syphilis syndrome, deafness or seizures may occur in some instances, but not all. With Coffin-Lowry syndrome (a rare genetic disorder typified by abnormalities of the head and face and the skeleton, short stature, low muscle tone and cognitive impairment), the cognitive impairment affects all males, but only a small percentage of females.

The number and severity of features may differ for different individuals with the same syndrome. Having considered aspects of syndromes in general we now turn to syndromes associated with cognitive impairment.

Some syndromes associated with cognitive impairment

The following section considers:

- Down syndrome
- Fragile X syndrome
- Prader-Willi syndrome
- Rett syndrome
- Fetal (or Foetal) alcohol syndrome
- Williams syndrome and
- Cri du Chat syndrome.

This list is by no means exhaustive, but is intended to provide a range of examples of syndromes that may give rise to cognitive impairment. The intention is also to show that general approaches for cognitive impairment are suitable, but that the other implications of syndrome also need to be taken into account when developing provision.

Down syndrome

Down syndrome gets its name from Langdon Down who in 1866 provided the first clear description of the condition. It is a genetic condition caused by a chromosomal abnormality, usually trisomy 21. It is not known what causes the chromosomal abnormality, but it occurs at conception. Individuals typically have 46 chromosomes, but individuals with Down syndrome have 47. Down syndrome occurs in about 1 in every 800 live births and is the commonest chromosome abnormality.

The condition is identified before birth or soon afterwards. Prenatal screening followed by diagnostic tests identifies Down syndrome before birth. There are physical indications such as a single crease across the palm of the hand and upwardly slanting eyes. The diagnosis is confirmed by carrying out an analysis of the chromosomes through examining blood or tissue cells.

The condition is associated with mild to moderate cognitive impairment. The child may also experience deafness, leukaemia or myopia (short sightedness). About three-quarters of individuals with Down syndrome have congenital heart disease (Candy, Davies and Ross, 2001, pp. 241–3). Echocardiograms are carried out on newly born babies with Down syndrome to establish if there are any cardiac problems. Sometimes these may require surgery, while in other instances they will require monitoring. This does not mean of course that every individual with Down syndrome will experience all of these associated difficulties.

Early assessment is important and this enables various therapies to be provided. These may include physical, speech and developmental therapies. Many children with Down syndrome attend regular schools either in ordinary classes or in special classes and some attend special schools. Provision in school includes ensuring the curriculum, pedagogy, resources, therapy, and school and classroom organisation are suitable for the level of cognitive impairment experienced. Schools also have to provide for any related health conditions. This involves ensuring close working with other professionals including as necessary physician, optician and audiologist. Such multi-professional working will concern initial and on-going assessments, and adjustments to educational provision.

Further information may be obtained at the National Association for Down Syndrome which predominantly serves the population of Chicago, Illinois, USA (www.nads.org) and at Down Syndrome Education International in the United Kingdom (www.dseinternational.org/en/gb/).

Fragile X syndrome

The broad term 'fragile X' is sometimes used for a group of genetic conditions that are brought about by changes in the same gene, the FMR1 gene found on the X chromosome. Fragile X syndrome is one of this group of conditions.

Fragile X syndrome is one of the commonest identifiable inherited causes of cognitive impairment. The 'fragile' part of the term refers to the seeming break at the end of the long arm of the X chromosome. The pattern of inheritance is X linked. A mother who is a carrier will pass on either a normal or an abnormal sex chromosome to her child. It follows that half of the number of male offspring will be affected and half of the number of female offspring will be carriers (Candy, Davies and Ross, 2001, p. 240).

The FMR1 gene is implicated in making a protein important in brain development and consequently there is an effect on brain function. Learning, behaviour and communication are affected.

Fragile X syndrome is associated with cognitive impairment and certain physical features, for example an elongated jaw and ears (Anderson, 2007, pp. 1855–6). Speech may be litany-like with up and down swings of pitch and rapid, dysrhythmic speech known as 'cluttering'. The child may avoid eye contact or injure himself for example through biting his hand when anxious or excited. His behaviour may be stereotyped and repetitive (Turk and Graham, 1997).

Effective provision involves adapting general approaches that work for cognitive impairment, autism and challenging behaviour. Where cognitive impairment is severe or profound, it is likely that assessment will involve small steps so that progress can be recognised and celebrated. Motor and language therapy are provided.

Further information is obtainable from the Fragile X Society based in the United Kingdom (www.fragilex.org.uk) and the National Fragile X Association based in the United States of America (www.nfxf.org).

Prader-Willi syndrome

Prader-Willi syndrome is a congenital condition named after the two Swiss paediatricians who first identified it, A. Prader and H. Willi. It results from an abnormality in the 15th chromosome. Estimates of prevalence vary, but the American website for the condition gives what is probably a sensible estimate of 1 in every 15,000 births.

It typically involves cognitive impairment, delay in speech and walking, under-developed genitals and excessive appetite. The child often develops diabetes mellitus. When the child wants food, he may exhibit challenging behaviour. The craving for food is coupled with lower use of calories than typical, so that the condition can lead to life-threatening obesity. Short stature is a feature unless it is treated with growth hormones.

Because the syndrome is associated with medical, nutritional, psychological, social, educational and therapeutic aspects, a range of professionals have to work closely together (Whittington and Holland, 2004). The educational provision takes into account the child's level of cognitive impairment. Supervision will be necessary to ensure the diet is adhered to. Physical education may not be the pupil's first choice of activity, so the teacher will need to ensure that the child's experience of physical education is positive and enjoyable. Further suggestions for the education of children with Prader-Willi syndrome may be found in the book *Prader-Willi Syndrome: A Practical Guide (Resource Materials for Teachers)* (Waters, 1999).

Further information is obtainable from the Prader-Willi Syndrome Association in the United Kingdom (www.pwsa.co.uk) and the Prader-Willi Syndrome Association in the United States of America (www.pwsausa.org).

Rett syndrome

Rett syndrome affects girls almost exclusively. It is named after the Austrian Andreas Rett who first described it in the 1960s. The condition was recognised medically in the 1980s. It is a rare condition affecting only about 1 in every 105,000 baby girls (Candy, Davies and Ross, 2001, p. 18). Rett syndrome is caused by a mutation on a gene located on the X chromosome.

Symptoms usually occur when the child is about 1 year to 18 months old after he or she has appeared to develop normally. Skills such as walking and talking that had previously been acquired begin to decline and the rate of the child's head growth also reduces. Cognition is impaired. Other characteristics are repeated hand movements and unexplained outbursts of laughter. The assessment of Rett syndrome based on symptoms can be confirmed by the molecular analysis of blood.

There is presently no cure. Individuals with the condition require constant care and attention.

Provision includes physical therapy, occupational therapy, and speech and language therapy. Medication may be prescribed such as anti-psychotic drugs to reduce self-harming. Children and young people with Rett syndrome can benefit from school and community activities, taking part in social, educational and recreational activities both at home and in the community.

Further reading includes *The Rett Syndrome Handbook* (Hunter, 2007). More information is obtainable from the International Rett Syndrome Association (www.rettsyndrome.org) and the UK-based Rett Syndrome Association (www.rettsyndrome.org.uk).

Fetal (or Foetal) alcohol syndrome

A link between alcohol consumed in pregnancy and impairments in babies was recognised before the 1970s. The term 'Fetal alcohol syndrome' was first used in 1973 in the United States of America by Kenneth Lyons Jones and David Weyhe Smith. They were dysmorphologists, that is, they studied congenital malformations in humans.

Fetal alcohol syndrome refers to a group of cognitive and physical impairments that develop in some unborn babies when their mother drinks alcohol to excess or at a critical time in pregnancy. Medical advice is that the mother should not drink alcohol at all if they are pregnant. The baby is affected because alcohol passes the placental barrier. This can lead to lower weight and growth and to physical, cognitive and behavioural problems. The nervous system, especially the brain, is affected. There are also certain facial features that are typical, such as a thin upper lip, a short nose and small eye openings.

Educational provision for children with fetal alcohol syndrome takes account of their level of cognitive impairment and other factors. Pedagogy will tend to be focused on what is practical and concrete. Behaviour may be difficult to manage as children with the syndrome may have difficulty relating cause and effect so that a strategy that worked to encourage behaviour on one occasion may be ineffective on another occasion. Where students have difficulties in maintaining attention, the teacher may need to be careful the classroom does not hold too many distractions. Some approaches used with children with attention deficit activity disorder may be useful, such as self-talk to help manage impulsive behaviour.

More information is available on the website of the National Organisation on Fetal Alcohol Syndrome (www.nofas-uk.org) based in the United Kingdom. In the United States of America, the website of the Minnesota Organisation on Fetal Alcohol Syndrome (www.mofas.org) provides more information. For further reading giving strategies, see *Fetal Alcohol Syndrome: A Guide for Families and Communities* (Streissguth, 1997).

Williams syndrome

Williams syndrome was first identified by J. C. P. Williams of New Zealand. It is sometimes known as Williams-Beuren syndrome. It is a developmental disorder caused by the deletion of genes from the long arm of chromosome 7. Facial signs associated with the condition include an elf-like appearance and a low nasal bridge. The child has developmental delay and language skills are affected. There may be cardiovascular problems. Many children with Williams syndrome are very verbal and sociable to such an extent that it is considered excessive. Estimates of the prevalence of Williams syndrome vary from about 1 in every 7,500 to 1 in every 20,000 live births. An average suggested by the Williams Syndrome Foundation (a UK-based charity) is about 1 in 25,000 live births.

Provision for children and young people with Williams syndrome takes account of cognitive impairment, which is usually mild to severe. Education can capitalise on relatively stronger spoken language and support poorer comprehension. Gross and fine motor problems are helped by cooperation with the physical therapist and the development of suitable programmes. Support is provided for visuo-spatial difficulties. The behavioural characteristics of children with Williams syndrome include that they tend to be overactive, have a shorter concentration span than peers, are sociable, may worry excessively, and may be very sensitive to sounds.

The school and classroom environment will take account of the child's particular learning and behavioural requirements. Teachers need to be careful to assess the child's abilities accurately and for example not overestimate other abilities on the basis of the child's fluency in language. Of course, neither must the teacher or others underestimate any abilities or interests.

Further reading includes *Understanding Williams Syndrome: Behavioural Patterns and Interventions* (Semel and Rosner, 2003). More information is available from the Williams Foundation in the United Kingdom (www. williams-syndrome.org.uk) and the Williams Foundation in the United States of America (www.wsf.org).

Cri du Chat syndrome

Cri du Chat syndrome is also called Lejeune syndrome. It is caused by the full or partial deletion of the short arm of chromosome 5. The short arms of chromosomes are labelled 'p' and the long arms are labelled 'q'. Therefore, the syndrome is also known as '5p syndrome' or 'deletion 5p syndrome'.

Features include low birth weight and slow growth, a cat-like cry in infancy, an abnormally small cranium (microcephaly), a round face with widely spaced eyes, facial asymmetry, squint, cognitive impairment, low set and poorly formed ears, untypical palm creases, variable congenital heart defect and epicanthic folds. (An epicanthic fold is a vertical fold of skin on the inner angle of the eye going from the upper eye-lid to the beginning of the nose.)

Provision includes ensuring the curriculum, pedagogy and other aspects are suited to cognitive impairment which is usually moderate to severe. A heart defect may have implications for the child's participation in sports and physical activities and how they are organised. The implications of a squint will be taken into account drawing on the advice of specialists. Similarly, any effects on hearing of the syndrome will be taken into account.

Further information is available at the website of the Cri du Chat Syndrome Support Group (www.criduchat.org.uk) in the United Kingdom or the 5p-society in the United States of America (www.fivepminus.org).

Other conditions associated with cognitive impairment

Various other conditions and factors may be associated with cognitive impairment. These include:

- phenylketonuria
- Tay-Sachs disease
- tuberous sclerosis.

Just as was the case when we considered syndromes, the conditions considered here are far from exhaustive. They are meant to offer various examples of conditions and factors that may give rise to cognitive impairment. The purpose of outlining these is also to show that general approaches for cognitive impairment are suitable, but that the other implications of conditions and factors need to be taken into account as well when you are developing provision.

Phenylketonuria

Phenylketonuria is known in Norway as Følling's disease after the Norwegian physician Ivar Asbjørn Følling who discovered the condition in 1943. Følling noticed that excessive phenylalanine (hyperphenylalaninia) is associated with cognitive impairment.

Phenylketonuria is an autosomal recessive metabolic genetic disorder. It involves a deficiency in a hepatic enzyme (phenylalanine hydroxylase). This enzyme is necessary to metabolise the amino acid phenylalanine to the amino acid tyrosine. When phenylalanine hydroxylase is deficient, phenylalanine accumulates. It is converted into phenylpyruvate which is detected in the urine, providing an indicator for the condition. Phenylketonuria is detected through screening new-born babies.

Although there is no cure, Phenylketonuria can be successfully managed by the individual, but if left untreated, it can affect brain development, leading to progressive cognitive impairment, brain damage and seizures. Treatment involves lowering blood phenylalanine levels and monitoring diet and cognitive development. Phenylalanine levels are lowered through a low-phenylalanine diet and protein supplements.

The school needs to work closely with parents and others to ensure dietary requirements are met. The curriculum, pedagogy and other aspects of provision will take account of the level of cognitive impairment experienced by the pupil.

Tay-Sachs disease

Tay-Sachs disease is a neurological genetic disorder that takes three forms (classic infantile, juvenile and late onset). It is named after Warren Tay, a British ophthalmologist who first clearly described a patient with a typical retinal sign; and Bernard Sachs, an American neurologist who later gave the first description of the cellular changes associated with the disease.

Tay-Sachs disease is brought about by a deficiency or a lack of an essential enzyme (hexosamidase). Without this enzyme, a fatty substance (lipid) known as GM2 ganglioside gathers abnormally in cells, particularly brain nerve cells, causing progressive damage. In classic infantile Tay-Sachs disease, the foetus is affected and symptoms become apparent when the child is several months old. By the age of 3 or 4 years old, it is difficult to sustain life, although some children with classic Tay-Sachs disease live longer.

Children who are affected begin to regress from the age of 5 months. Individuals tend to react in a startled way to noise. There is no treatment and the condition generally leads to death in early adulthood (Candy, Davies and Ross, 2001, p. 290). Active research is taking place to look for therapeutic drug interventions.

Further information is available from the National Tay-Sachs and Allied Diseases Association Incorporated based in the United States of America (www.ntsad.org).

Tuberous sclerosis

Tuberous sclerosis is a term used in the United States of America. In the United Kingdom, it is often called tuberose sclerosis. Potato-shaped degenerative swellings develop in the brain, hence the name. The condition also causes the deposition of abnormal tissue in the eyes, bones and elsewhere. Where the abnormal depositing of tissue affects the skin, several patches of milky coffee coloured staining may appear. Over the cheeks there may be patches of reddened thick tissues rather like acne. Prevalence is estimated to be about 1 in every 6,000 live births.

Many individuals with tuberous sclerosis are little affected. Severely affected individuals tend to have cognitive impairment and epilepsy (Candy, Davies and Ross, 2001, p. 325). In school, teachers need to provide for any cognitive impairment. You also need to be trained in seizure first aid for children who have epilepsy. Training in awareness of other health issues that may arise is also important. Where the child is on a special diet, it is important this is adhered to and there is good liaison with parents about this and other matters.

Further information may be obtained from the Tuberous Sclerosis Association, based in the United Kingdom (www.tuberous-sclerosis. org) and the Tuberous Sclerosis Alliance in the United States of America (www.tsalliance.org).

Further factors associated with cognitive impairment

Various other factors may be associated with cognitive impairment. These include:

- iodine deficiency
- hypoxia
- social and family circumstances.

Iodine deficiency

Iodine is an essential non-metallic chemical element. It is found in sea water and in certain minerals. It is important to ensure the development and release of thyroid hormones. These are vital to promoting a range of cognitive and bodily processes. Iodine helps synthesise thyroid hormones that help regulate bodily growth, development, metabolism and body temperature.

In consequence, where there is insufficient iodine in the diet, this can lead to health problems and cognitive impairment. Worldwide, iodine deficiency is the most common cause of preventable mental impairment (Zimmerman, Jooste and Pandav, 2008). Iodine deficiency adversely affects growth and development owing to the inadequate production of thyroid hormone. It causes the gradual enlargement of the thyroid gland – a condition known as goitre.

Where a pregnant woman has insufficient iodine in her diet, this can increase the risk of the child being born with cognitive impairments.

Iodine deficiency is assessed in various ways, including checking the concentration of iodine in the urine. The most successful strategy to control iodine deficiency is the iodisation of salt or failing that providing susceptible groups with iodine supplements (Zimmerman, Jooste and Pandav, 2008).

Hypoxia

Hypoxia refers to asphyxia around the time of a baby's birth, that is, insufficient oxygen. The brain can be affected and permanent damage can occur. There are several causes of interference with the blood supply to the foetus resulting in asphyxia.

For example, before labour, blood supply to the placenta may be insufficient over a prolonged period of time. During labour, the umbilical cord may be overly compressed. At birth, blood may be lost from the cord, or congenital defects such as to the baby's heart can lead to lack of oxygen (Candy, Davies and Ross, 2001, pp. 27–8).

Where the brain is affected this can lead to varying degrees of cognitive impairment and the teacher and school provide for this depending on its severity.

Social and family circumstances

When we considered causal factors in an earlier chapter, I indicated that there was debate about whether 'mild cognitive impairment' can be considered a condition in the way for example that Down syndrome can. Individual factors and environmental factors may be involved or a combination of the two in varying degrees. Intelligence tests and assessments of functioning may be taken to indicate individual factors. Poor social, cultural and economic background can be influential.

Low attainment may not be the result of 'mild cognitive impairment', but may relate to home and family circumstances that, if changed, might lead to the child making better progress and attaining better, perhaps age typical, levels. Alternatively, home and family circumstances (and other factors) may be considered to have influenced the child's cognitive development such that even if family circumstances were to change, there would still be evidence of mild cognitive impairment (see also Baroff, 1999, pp. 202–37).

Whatever the balance of judgement about the relative contribution of social and family circumstances and whatever the view about the extent they may have led to within child cognitive impairment, the practical implications are similar. These include supporting the whole family to ensure the best environment in which the child can learn and develop. This support lies beyond what might reasonably be expected of a school and will involve other agencies too. The school may offer particular help with family literacy if parents and siblings are unable to read well. Provision for breakfast before school starts and opportunities for activities after school may be offered.

Challenging behaviour

The nature of challenging behaviour

Where challenging behaviour occurs, it tends to be associated with profound cognitive impairment rather than mild, moderate or severe cognitive impairment. Some conditions, for example Rett syndrome, tend to be associated with challenging behaviour as already indicated. Even so, this is not to suggest that all pupils with profound cognitive impairment exhibit challenging behaviour. Neither is behaviour that challenges staff, pupils and others exclusive to pupils with profound cognitive impairment.

But there are particular challenges to parents and professionals managing such behaviours where a child also has profound cognitive impairment. For example, the child may have difficulties communicating what he wants to other people. It may be difficult for the child to comprehend that some behaviours are harmful or in other ways undesirable.

Also, the context of profound cognitive impairment influences the range of interventions that can be effective. Consider interventions used with students with opposition defiant disorder, conduct disorder, anxiety disorder, depressive disorder and attention hyperactivity disorder. (These are described in the book in this series *The Effective Teacher's Guide to Behavioural and Emotional Disorders: Disruptive Behaviour Disorders, Anxiety Disorders and Depressive Disorders, and Attention Deficit Hyperactivity Disorder*). It is not possible simply to take these interventions and apply them to a student with profound cognitive impairment. Many of the interventions assume that the student has average or above levels of intelligence and age-typical communication skills and can make sense of and reflect on behaviour and thoughts. Interventions for a student with profound cognitive impairment have to take into account that he cannot make sense of the world in the same way as many students with for example conduct disorder.

Teachers, physicians, parents and other professionals do not always agree what constitutes challenging behaviour. There are several reasons for this. Standards of what is acceptable may differ according to social class, culture, different chronological and developmental ages of children and different settings. Sometimes parents and professionals cannot agree among themselves that challenging behaviour is evident. This can be because of different interpretations of particular behaviour or conflicting views about its severity.

I take the view for present purposes that challenging behaviour is behaviour that is socially unacceptable and significantly blocks learning. The behaviour is likely to be intense, frequent or long lasting. Because of this the safety of the person exhibiting the behaviour or that of those around him is at risk. Such behaviour is likely to limit access to community facilities. In the short term, challenging behaviour may prohibit community access altogether. Challenging behaviour includes aggression, self-injury, stereotyped behaviour and problematic sexual behaviour (Olley in Baroff, 1999, pp. 370–95).

Some examples may illustrate the range of behaviour that may be considered challenging. It may include:

- injury to oneself or to others;
- damage to surroundings;
- severe lack of compliance;
- repeated absconding;
- stereotyped speech or movement;
- faecal smearing;
- habitually eating substances other than food such as paper or dirt (this habit is also known as pica);
- inappropriate sexual behaviour (for example public masturbation or exposing the genitals to others);
- persistent screaming;
- repeated vomiting; and
- extreme hyperactivity.

Causal and sustaining factors

In some cases challenging behaviour is linked to particular conditions such as Lesch–Nyhan syndrome. This is associated with self-injurious behaviour and often violence to others, spitting and vomiting (Goldstein and Reynolds, 1999 provide a fuller description). Other factors that can contribute to challenging behaviour are the side effects of drugs, pain, stress, anxiety and depression. Further reasons include being unable to convey basic needs. The effect of phobias may be to give rise to challenging behaviour. The child may have limited language and understanding. He may be intolerant of perceived over stimulation. A low boredom threshold; discomfort from physical impairment or incontinence; and insecurity because of sensory impairment are further potential causes of challenging behaviour.

Challenging behaviour may be a way for the child or young person to communicate. This suggests the importance of individual communication programmes devised in conjunction with a speech and language pathologist/therapist. Challenging behaviour may be used to communicate a request for social activities such as attention or interaction. It may indicate a request for items such as food or a toy; a protest or refusal to comply with a request; or a wish to escape from a situation. It may indicate dissatisfaction; a comment or declaration such as a greeting or compliance with a request; or boredom, pain or tiredness.

Given these possible motivations and reasons, it is essential that the teacher and others analyse the possible communicative function of challenging behaviour. In this way effective interventions can be developed. These interventions may relate to consequences or antecedents of the challenging behaviour which may be sustaining the behaviour.

Assessment of challenging behaviour

One approach is functional behavioural assessment. This form of assessment is outlined in the website of the American Institute for Research (AIR) Center for Effective Collaboration and Practice (CECP) (http://cecp.air.org). Further details are provided by Crone and Horner (2003).

Functional behavioural assessment is a problem-solving process for tackling pupils' problem behaviour. It attempts to identify the purpose of the behaviour and find ways to intervene to address it. Factors are considered which influence the behaviour: social, affective, cognitive and environmental. Behavioural interventions are informed by the apparent reasons for the behaviour. In this way, purpose and function of the challenging behaviour for the child can be better understood.

Provision for challenging behaviour

In school, you will try with colleagues to create an optimal learning environment for children with challenging behaviour. A multi-disciplinary team will work with parents to develop intervention programmes. These will take into consideration medical care and the child's or young person's developmental level. Specific programmes are individually plan-ned, systematically implemented and rigorously assessed. Based on this, the programmes are modified or changed if they are not having the desired effect.

Interventions may relate to functional analysis. To eliminate challenging behaviour in the longer term, more suitable alternative behaviour will need to be supported by naturally occurring events reinforcing the new behaviour. One way of ensuring natural contingencies are applied is to teach new functional behaviours. These must result in reinforcing con-sequences similar to those available following the unwanted behaviour. Also, the new behaviour must be reinforced by the same consequences that reinforced the unwanted behaviour.

Successful intervention depends on expanding the limited response repertoires of individuals with cognitive impairment. It is not just a matter of trying to eliminate the inappropriate behaviour. Some inter-ventions are designed to teach new communicative behaviours to replace unwanted behaviour. You may teach a child desiring food to use a non-verbal sign rather than be disruptive. Other interventions are developed to teach alternative functionally related behaviour to replace unwanted behaviour. You might teach the child to listen to peaceful music on a headset to suppress an over-stimulating environment as an alternative to the child shrieking.

Yet other interventions involve changing the events leading up to the inappropriate behaviour. Consider your observations indicate that the child's unwanted behaviour suggests a wish to escape from a demanding activity. You might simplify the tasks and use errorless learning to try to reduce the child's wish to avoid the activity. Children with challenging behaviour may need from time to time additional staff or equipment, or a modified timetable. Where special behavioural programmes are devised, you may need support and advice from a psychologist who specialises in developing and implementing behavioural interventions. See also the chapter by Olley in Baroff (1999, pp. 359–95).

General considerations regarding syndromes and conditions and cognitive impairment

Having examined a range of conditions that can be associated with cognitive impairment, it may be helpful to reassert the relationship between such conditions and special education.

In developing suitable provision for a child with a disability or disorders several factors are taken into account. The first is that provision that is suitable and important for all children is provided. This includes human warmth, emotional support, physical care and so on. This of course is provided whether or not a child has a disability or disorder. Second, provision takes account of what is individual to any particular child. This will include his preferences, the best ways he learns, his interests and so on. Teachers and others learn these from getting to know individual children. Again, individual differences are important whether or not the child has a disability or disorder. The third set of factors concern what is general about provision for certain disabilities and disorders.

It is this third set of factors that is the subject of special education. Rather than start from scratch every time she educated a child with profound cognitive impairment, a teacher will remember the provision in terms of curriculum, pedagogy, resources, therapy and school and classroom organisation that tends to be effective with profound cognitive impairment.

In one sense, provision may be no different for a child with profound cognitive impairment whether the impairment was brought about by one condition or another.

In another sense, the particular condition may inform the responses that are necessary to ensure the best education. For example, a child with Rett syndrome may benefit from provision typical for children with say severe cognitive impairment. But provision is also likely to include physical therapy, occupational therapy, and speech and language therapy and may include the prescribing of anti-psychotic drugs to reduce self-harm. This is partly responding to individual requirements that may be different for different children with Rett syndrome. The educator still needs to respond to the individual requirements specific to an individual child.

In brief then the educators need to know about the general approaches to different levels of cognitive impartment. These were presented in earlier chapters in terms of mild cognitive impairment, moderate to severe cognitive impartments, and profound cognitive impairment. You also need to be aware of likely features of particular conditions that have led to cognitive impairments so that other features of the condition are provided for. You also of course need to respond to the child's individual requirements and the general requirements that are important for all children.

Thinking points

Readers may wish to consider with reference to a particular school:

- the provision made for children with syndromes and other conditions whose features include cognitive impairment;

- how effectively the school provides for the requirements that arise from the syndrome or condition other than cognitive impairment; and
- the provision made for children whose cognitive impairment may relate to other factors, including poor social and family environment.

Key texts

Candy, D., Davies, G. and Ross, E. (2001) *Clinical Paediatrics and Child Health* Edinburgh, London and New York, Saunders Elsevier

This provides basic medical information relating to a range of conditions, some of which are associated with cognitive impairment.

Dykens, E. M., Hodapp, R. M. and Finucane, B. M. (2000) *Genetics and Mental Retardation Syndromes: A New Look at Behaviour and Interventions* Baltimore, MD, Paul H. Brookes

This text identifies characteristics of various syndromes and related interventions.

Gilbert, P. (2000) *A to Z of Syndromes and Inherited Disorders* London, Stanley Thornes

As the title indicates, this book covers a wide range of syndromes and disorders.

Chapter 6

Summary and conclusion

The book has considered several types of disability and disorder:

- mild cognitive impairment/moderate learning difficulties;
- moderate to severe cognitive impairment/severe learning difficulties;
- profound cognitive impairment/profound learning difficulties; and
- various syndromes, conditions and factors associated with cognitive impairment.

We also looked at challenging behaviour.

For each range of cognitive impairment it was maintained that there are particular implications for provision. This was considered in terms of:

- the curriculum and assessment
- pedagogy
- resources
- school and classroom organisation and
- therapy and care.

Mild cognitive impairment/moderate learning difficulties

I outlined the debate about the relative contribution of within child and environmental contributions to mild cognitive impairment. Definitions, prevalence, causal factors, and identification and assessment were examined. Under provision, I looked at: curriculum and assessment; pedagogy; resources; therapy and organisation. Regarding pedagogy, key areas were: communication; literacy and numeracy; behavioural, emotional and social development; slower but stimulating pace; concrete learning; and ensuring relevance and generalisation.

Moderate to severe cognitive impairment/severe learning difficulties

With reference to moderate and severe cognitive impairment, we looked at definitions, prevalence, causal factors and identification and assessment. Regarding provision, we examined: curriculum, including cross-curricular links, and assessment; pedagogy resources; therapy; and organisation. Suitable pedagogy included focusing on visual inputs, communication, developing autonomy and independence, and community-based vocational instruction.

Profound cognitive impairment/profound learning difficulties

Regarding profound cognitive impairment, I looked at definitions, prevalence, causal factors and identification and assessment. Curriculum requirements included sensory elements and finely graded assessment. Pedagogy included attention to communication, task-analytic instruction, multi-sensory approaches and daily living experiences, and community-based vocational instruction. The development of a responsive environment was also discussed. Suitable resources and therapy were also mentioned.

Various conditions associated with cognitive impairment

In this chapter we looked at examples of syndromes, conditions and other factors associated with cognitive impairment and considered how broad approaches for different levels of cognitive impairment are shaped and added to where particular conditions and factors indicate. Aspects of challenging behaviour were examined as well as strategies to encourage appropriate behaviour.

A final word

The above summary of provision for different types of disabilities and disorders that have been examined in this book indicates the importance to schools of reviewing their curriculum, pedagogy, resources, organisation and therapy. In doing so, schools will be able to ensure that provision helps encourage the best academic progress and the best personal and social development for its pupils.

Another essential aspect of special education that has been implicit throughout the book is that of professionals working closely with parents and other professionals. It is helpful to recognise the importance of professional contributions and the foundational disciplines that contribute to special education. Examples of these foundational disciplines are:

- legal/typological
- terminological
- social
- medical
- neuropsychological
- psychotherapeutic
- behavioural/observational
- developmental
- psycholinguistic
- technological
- pedagogical.

Legal/typological foundations of special education concern social, political and economic factors informing the context of special education legislation. It includes an understanding of current legislation and the main types of disabilities and disorders drawing on classifications used in the systems in the country concerned. Terminological matters include the importance of terminology in special education, for example, 'needs', 'discrimination' and 'rights'. Social foundations include a social constructionist perspective. A social view of disability has been important in widening the understanding beyond individual factors. Medical influences involve the scope of the application of medical perspectives and the use of drugs in relation to children with disabilities and disorders.

Neuropsychological aspects draw on techniques used in neurological research and some uses of psychological and related tests in neuropsychology. Psychotherapeutic contributions involve systems, psychodynamic and cognitive-behavioural approaches. Behavioural and observational foundations consider behavioural approaches to learning with reference to learning theory and observational learning and modelling in social cognitive theory. Developmental features may draw on Piaget's theory of genetic epistemology, for example, in relation to understandings of provision for children with cognitive impairment.

Psycholinguistic foundations involve frameworks incorporating input processing, lexical representations and output processing, and interventions. Technological aspects may explore how technology constitutes a foundation of special education through its enhancement of teaching and learning. Pedagogical aspects examine pedagogy in relation to special education, in particular the issue of distinctive pedagogy for different types of disabilities and disorders.

The book *Foundations of Special Education* (Farrell, 2009a) discusses these areas in detail.

Bibliography

Abbeduto, L. and Hesketh, L. J. (1997) 'Pragmatic development in individuals with mental retardation: Learning to use language in social interactions' *Mental Retardation and Developmental Disabilities Research Reviews* 3, 323–33.

Aird, R. (2001) *The Education and Care of Children with Severe, Profound and Multiple Learning Difficulties* London, David Fulton Publishers.

Algozzine, B. and Ysseldyke, E. (2006) *Teaching Students with Mental Retardation: A Practical Guide for Teachers* Thousand Oaks, CA, Corwin Press.

Alton, S. (2001) 'Children with Down's syndrome and short term auditory memory' *Down's Syndrome Association Journal* 95, (Winter) 4–9.

American Psychiatric Association (2000) *Diagnostic and Statistical Manual of Mental Disorders Fourth Edition Text Revision (DSM-IV-TR)* Washington DC, APA.

Anderson, D. M. (Chief lexicographer) (2007) (31st edition) *Dorland's Illustrated Medical Dictionary* Philadelphia, PA, Elsevier/Saunders.

Arvio, M. and Sillanpaa, M. (2003) 'Prevalence, aetiology and comorbidity of severe and profound intellectual disability in Finland' *Journal of Intellectual Disability Research* 47, 2, 108–12.

Baroff, G. S. with Olley, J. G. (1999) (3rd edition) *Mental Retardation: Nature, Causes and Management* Philadelphia, PA, Brunner/Mazel.

Bigge, J. L., Best, S. J. and Heller, K. W. (2001) (4th edition) *Teaching Individuals with Physical, Health or Multiple Disabilities* Upper Saddle River, NJ, Merrill-Prentice Hall.

Borkowski, J. G., Chan, L. K. S. and Muthukrishna, N. (2000) 'A process-oriented model of metacognition: Links between motivation and executive functioning' in Schraw, G. and Impara, J. C. (Eds) *Issues in the Measurement of Metacognition* (pp. 1–41) Lincoln, NE, Buros Institute of Mental Measurements.

Borkowski, J. G., Carothers, S. S., Howard, K., Schatz, J. and Farris, J. (2006) 'Intellectual assessment and intellectual disability' in Jacobson, J. W., Mulick, J. A. and Rojhan, J. (Eds) *Handbook of Mental Retardation and Developmental Abilities* New York, Springer.

Bransford, J. D., Delclos, V. R., Vye, N. J., Burns, M. S. and Hasselbring, T. S. (1986) 'State of the art and future direction' in Lidz, C. S. (Ed.) *Dynamic Assessment:*

An Interactional Approach to Evaluating Learning Potential (pp. 479–96) New York, Guilford Press.

Brooks, G. (2002) *What Works for Reading Difficulties? The Effectiveness of Intervention Schemes* London, Department of Education and Science.

Butler, F. M., Miller, S. P., Lee, K. and Pierce, T. (2001) 'Teaching mathematics to students with mild to moderate mental retardation: A review of the literature' *Mental Retardation* 39, 1, 20–31.

Candy, D., Davies, G. and Ross, E. (2001) *Clinical Paediatrics and Child Health* Edinburgh, London and New York, Saunders Elsevier.

Carpenter, B. (1994) 'Finding a home for the sensory curriculum' *PMLD Link* 19, 2–3.

Carr, A. (2006) (2nd edition) *The Handbook of Child and Adolescent Clinical Psychology: A Contextual Approach* London, Routledge.

Carter, M. and Grunsell, J. (2001) 'The behaviour chain interruption strategy: A review of research and discussion of future directions' *Journal for the Association of the Severely Handicapped* 26, 1, 37–49.

Copeland, S. R. and Hughes, C. (2000) 'Acquisition of a picture prompt strategy to increase independent performance' *Education and Training in Mental Retardation and Developmental Disabilities* 35, 3, 294–305.

Cornish, U. and Ross, F. (2003) *Social Skills Training for Adolescents with General Moderate Learning Difficulties* London, Jessica Kingsley Publishers.

Crocker, A. C. (1992) 'Human immunodeficiency virus' In Levine, M. D., Carey, W. B. and Crocker, A. C. (Eds) *Developmental-Behavioural Paediatrics* (271–5) Philadelphia, PA, W. B. Saunders.

Crone, D. A. and Horner, R. H. (2003) *Building Positive Behaviour Support Systems in Schools: Functional Behavioural Assessment* New York, Guilford Press.

Day, J. (1995) (2nd edition) *Access Technology: Making the Right Choice* Coventry, National Council for Educational Technology.

Department for Education and Skills (DfES) (2005) (2nd edition) *Data Collection by Special Educational Need* London, DfES.

Detheridge, T. and Stevens, C. (2001) 'Information and communication technology' in Carpenter, B., Ashdown, R. and Bovair, K. (Eds) *Enabling Access: Effective Teaching and Learning for Pupils with Learning Difficulties* (pp. 156–69) London, David Fulton Publishers.

Drew, C. J. and Hardman, M. L. (2006) (9th edition) *Intellectual Disabilities across the Lifespan* Upper Saddle River, NJ, Prentice Hall.

Dykens, E. M., Hodapp, R. M. and Finucane, B. M. (2000) *Genetics and Mental Retardation Syndromes: A New Look at Behaviour and Interventions* Baltimore, MD, Paul H. Brookes.

Evans, P. and Ware, J. (1987) *Special Care Provision* Windsor, NFER-Nelson.

Farrell, M. (2006) *Celebrating the Special School* London, David Fulton Publishers.

——(2009a) *Foundations of Special Education: An Introduction* Chichester, West Sussex, UK, Wiley-Blackwell.

——(2009b) (4th edition) *The Special Education Handbook: An A–Z Guide* London, David Fulton Publishers.

Fujiki, M., Brinton, B. and Clarke, D. (2002) 'Emotion regulation in children with specific language impairment' *Language, Speech, and Hearing Services in Schools* 33, 102–11.

Gilbert, P. (2000) *A to Z of Syndromes and Inherited Disorders* London, Stanley Thornes.

Gillberg, C. and Soderstrom, H. (2003) 'Learning disability' *The Lancet* 362, 8711–821.

Goldstein, S. and Reynolds, C. R. (Eds) (1999) *Handbook of Neurodevelopmental and Genetic Disorders in Children* New York, NY, Guilford Press.

Greenspan, S. (2006) 'Functional concepts in mental retardation: Finding the natural essence of an artificial category' *Exceptionality* 14, 4, 205–24.

Guess, D., Siegel-Causey, E., Roberts, S., Rues, J., Thompson, B. and Siegel-Causey, D. (1990) 'Assessment and analysis of behavioural state and related variables among students with profoundly handicapping conditions' *Journal of the Association for Persons with Severe Handicaps* 15, 211–30.

Hatcher, P. (2000) 'Sound links in reading and spelling with discrepancy defined dyslexics and children with moderate learning difficulties' *Reading and Writing: An Interdisciplinary Journal* 13, 257–72.

Henry, L. C. and Maclean, M. (2002) 'Working memory performance in children with and without intellectual disabilities' *American Journal on Mental Retardation* 107, 6, 421–32.

Hewett, D. and Nind, M. (1998) *Interaction in Action* London, David Fulton Publishers.

Hodapp, R. M. and Dykens, E. M. (1994) 'Mental retardation's two cultures of behavioural research' *American Journal on Mental Retardation* 98, 6, 675–87.

Hodges, L. (2000) 'Effective teaching and learning' in Aitken, S., Buultjens, M. and Clark, C. et al. (Eds) *Teaching Children Who Are Deafblind: Contact, Communication and Learning* London, David Fulton Publishers.

Hunter, K. (2007) (2nd edition) *The Rett Syndrome Handbook* Clinton, MD, International Rett Syndrome Association Publishing.

Kauffman, J. M. and Hallahan, D. P. (2005) *Special Education: What It Is and Why We Need It* Boston, MA, Pearson/Allyn and Bacon.

Kaufman, A. S. and Kaufman, N. L. (2004) *KABC-II Administration and Scoring Manual* Circle Pines, MN, American Guidance Service.

King-de Baun, P. (1990) *Storytime: Stories, Symbols and Emergent Literacy Activities for Young Special Needs Children* Park City UT, Creative Communicating.

Kushlick, A. and Blunden, R. (1974) 'The epidemiology of mental subnormality' in Clarke, A. M. and Clarke, A. D. B. (Eds) (3rd edition) *Mental Deficiency* London, Methuen.

Lacey, P. (1991) 'Managing the classroom environment' in Tilstone, C. (Ed.) *Teaching Pupils with Severe Learning Difficulties* London, David Fulton Publishers.

Lancioni, G. E., O'Reilly, M. F., Oliva, D., Singh, N. N. and Coppa, M. M. (2002) 'Multiple microswitches for multiple responses with children with profound disabilities' *Cognitive Behaviour Therapy* 31, 2, 81–7.

Light, J. (1989) 'Towards a definition of communicative competence for individuals using augmentative and alternative communication systems' *Augmentative and Alternative Communication* 5, 134–7.

MacKay, G. (2002) 'The disappearance of disability? Thoughts on a changing culture' *British Journal of Special Education* 29, 4.

Male, D. (1996) 'Who goes to special schools?' *British Journal of Special Education* 23, 1, 35–41.

McDonnell, J., Hardman, M. L., Hightower, J., Keifer-O'Donnell, R. and Drew, C. (1993) 'Impact of community based instruction on the development of adaptive behaviour of secondary level students with mental retardation' *American Journal on Mental Retardation* 97, 5, 575–84.

Mar, H. M. and Sall, N. (1999) 'Profiles of the expressive communication skills of children and adolescents with severe cognitive disabilities' *Education and Training in Mental Retardation and Developmental Disabilities* 34, 1, 77–89.

Meese, R. L. (2001) (2nd edition) *Teaching Learners with Mild Disabilities: Integrating Research and Practice* Belmont, CA, Wadsworth-Thompson.

Morra, S., Gobbo, C., Marini, Z. and Sheese, R. (2007) *Cognitive Development: Neo Piagetian Perspectives* Mahwah, NJ, Lawrence Erlbaum Associates.

Norwich, B. and Kelly, N. (2004) *Moderate Learning Difficulties and the Future of Inclusion* London, Routledge Falmer.

Nind, M. and Hewett, D. (2001) *A Practical Guide to Intensive Interaction* Kidderminster, British Institute of Learning Difficulties.

Nind, M. and Kellett, M. (2002) 'Responding to individuals with severe learning difficulties and stereotyped behaviour: challenges for an inclusive era' *European Journal of Special Needs Education* 17, 3, 265–82.

Olley, J. G. (1999) 'Chapter 9: Maladaptive or "Challenging Behaviour": Its Nature and Treatment' in Baroff, J. S. with Olley, J. G. (1999) (3rd edition) *Mental Retardation: Nature, Cause and Management* Philadelphia, PA, Brunner/Mazel.

Ouvry, C. and Saunders, S. (2001) 'Pupils with profound and multiple learning difficulties' in Carpenter, B., Ashdown, R. and Bovair, K. (Eds) (2001) *Enabling Access: Effective Teaching and Learning for Pupils with Learning Difficulties* (pp. 240–56) London, David Fulton Publishers.

Panter, S. (2001) 'Mathematics' in Carpenter, B., Ashdown, R. and Bovair, K. (Eds) (2001) (2nd edition) *Enabling Access: Effective Teaching and Learning for Pupils with Learning Difficulties* (pp. 36–51) London, David Fulton Publishers.

Pease, L. (2000) 'Creating a communicating environment' in Aitken, S., Buultjens, M. and Clark, C. et al. (Eds) (2000) *Teaching Children Who Are Deafblind: Contact, Communication and Learning* London, David Fulton Publishers.

Piaget, J. and Inhelder, B. (1966/1969) *The Psychology of the Child* London, Routledge and Keegan Paul (trans. by Weaver, H.).

Pintrich, P. R. (2000) 'The role of goal orientation in self-regulated learning' in Boekaerts, M., Pintrich, P. R. and Zeider, M. (Eds) *Handbook of Self-Regulation* (pp. 452–502) New York, Academic.

Qualifications and Curriculum Authority (2001a) *Planning, Teaching and Assessing the Curriculum for Pupils with Learning Difficulties: English* London, QCA.

——(2001b) *Planning, Teaching and Assessing the Curriculum for Pupils with Learning Difficulties: Mathematics* London, QCA.

——(2001c) *Planning, Teaching and Assessing the Curriculum for Pupils with Learning Difficulties: Personal, Social and Health Education and Citizenship* London, QCA.

Reynolds, C. R. and Fletcher-Janzen, E. (Eds) (2004) (2nd edition) *Concise Encyclopaedia of Special Education: A Reference for the Education of Handicapped and Other Exceptional Children and Adults* Hoboken, NY, John Wiley & Sons.

Rinaldi, W. (2001) *Social Use of Language Programme* Windsor, NFER-Nelson.

Rumeau-Rouquette, C., du Mazaubrun, C. and Cans, C. et al. (1998) 'Definition and prevalence of school-age multi-handicaps' *Archives of Paediatric and Adolescent Medicine* 5, 7, 739–44.

Semel, E. and Rosner, S. R. (2003) *Understanding Williams Syndrome: Behavioural Patterns and Interventions* Mahwah, NJ, Lawrence Erlbaum Associates, Inc.

Sparrow, S. S., Chicchetti, D. V. and Balla, D. A. (2006) (2nd edition) *Vineland Adaptive Behaviour Scales* (Vineland II), Circle Pines, Minnesota, Pearson Assessments.

Streissguth, A. P. (1997) *Fetal Alcohol Syndrome: A Guide for Families and Communities* Baltimore, MD, Paul H. Brookes.

Stright, A. D. and Supplee, L. H. (2002) 'Children's self-regulatory behaviours during teacher-directed, seat-work, and small-group instructional contexts' *Journal of Education Research* 95, 235–45.

Switzky, H. N. and Greenspan, S. (2006) (Eds) *What Is Mental Retardation? Ideas for an Evolving Disability in the 21st Century* Washington, DC, American Association on Intellectual and Developmental Disabilities.

Turk, J. and Graham, P. (1997) 'Fragile X syndrome, autism and autistic features' *Autism* 1, 175–97.

Turner, J. C. (1995) 'The influence of classroom contexts on young children's motivation for literacy' *Reading Research Quarterly* 30, 410–41.

Vygotsky, L. S. ([1930 and various dates]/1978) *Mind in Society: Development of Higher Psychological Processes* Harvard, MA, Harvard University Press.

Ware, J. (2005) 'Profound and multiple learning difficulties' in Lewis, A. and Norwich, B. (Eds) *Special Teaching for Special Children? Pedagogies for Inclusion* Maidenhead, Open University Press.

Waters, J. (1999) *Prader-Willi Syndrome: A Practical Guide (Resource Materials for Teachers)* London, David Fulton Publishers.

Watson, J. and Fisher, A. (1997) 'Evaluating the effectiveness of Intensive Interactive teaching with pupils with profound and complex learning difficulties' *British Journal of Special Education* 24, 2, 80–87.

Wechsler, D. (1991) *Wechsler Intelligence Scale for Children – Third Edition* San Antonio, TX, Psychological Corporation.

——(2003) *Wechsler Intelligence Scale for Children – Fourth Edition (WISC-IV)* San Antonio, TX, Psychological Corporation.

Wehmeyer, M. L. with Sands, D. J., Knowlton, H. E. and Kozleski, E. B. (2002) *Providing Access to the General Curriculum: Teaching Students with Mental Retardation* Baltimore, MD, Paul H. Brookes.

Wellesley, D., Hockey, K., Montgomery, P. and Stanley, F. (1992) 'Prevalence of intellectual handicap in Western Australia: A community study' *Medical Journal of Australia* 156, 2, 94–6, 100, 102.

Whittington, J. and Holland, T. (2004) *Prader-Willi Syndrome: Developments and Manifestations* Cambridge, Cambridge University Press.

Wilson, J. and Frederickson, N. (1995) 'Phonological awareness training: an evaluation' *Educational and Child Psychology* 12, 1, 68–79.

Zimmerman, M. B., Jooste, P. L. and Pandav, C. S. (2008) 'Iodine-deficiency disorders' *The Lancet* 372(9645), 1251–62, October.

Index